"*Shattering Silence* is Darlene Lekowski's unflinching account of the strength, vulnerability, and lasting impact of childhood sibling sexual assault and trauma. With raw honesty and emotional clarity, she reveals how trauma extends far beyond the body, shaping every corner of a survivor's life. . . . As Lekowski shares the many stages of her survival and recovery, readers are given a rare and powerful glimpse into the complexities of healing and the courage it takes to claim one's voice."

—CINDY HANIG, LCSW

"Darlene's story is a compelling mix of heart warming memories and gut-wrenching experiences. She was raw and honest throughout. I was intrigued watching a little girl grow up on the pages, while frustrated that I could not reach into those pages to help her. . . . Her story is an important reminder of the person behind the client who hires us attorneys to guide them through the judicial system. And, the necessity of caring and having compassion for those clients we have the privilege of representing. Afterall, providing justice for our clients is at the heart of why we became attorneys in the first place."

—JEFF KUYKENDAL, attorney, MGC Law Firm

"In *Shattering Silence*, Darlene Lekowski takes an unflinching look at the abuse she experienced from two of her brothers. This powerful and moving memoir takes on sibling sexual abuse in all its complexity, its impact on family relationships, and the struggle to achieve justice. It is the story of Darlene's strength and her determination not to let her experience ruin her family or her life. You can't help rooting for little Darlene, who is stronger than any child should have to be."

—TANYA ROULEAU WHITWORTH, PHD,
Sibling Aggression and Abuse Research and
Advocacy Initiative at the University of New Hampshire

"*Shattering Silence* is a brave and unvarnished telling of a life lived under the weight of secrets. Darlene writes to give her younger self a voice, and in doing so offers a hand to others who have carried similar burdens alone. What stays with me is her shift from seeking justice outside herself to finding her inner power. The memoir is raw in places, tender in others, and always honest. A powerful story from a woman reclaiming her own truth."

—ALICE PERLE, author of *Resolve*

"Darlene Lekowski is nothing short of a twenty-first-century heroine who reminds us that when one woman rises, she lifts countless others with her. This is a brave and haunting book that will deeply resonate with anyone whose voice has been silenced but longs to stand tall, proud, and loud."

—NANCY SHARP, author of *Both Sides Now: A True Story of Love, Loss, and Bold Living*

"*Shattering Silence* gives a perspective and a resolve which proves that with courage and intention, anything is possible, and we do not need to be defined by our past."

—RICH NISBET, Above It All 360 counselor and life coach

SHATTERING
SILENCE

SHATTERING SILENCE

A Story of Survival, Justice, and the Power of Telling the Truth

DARLENE LEKOWSKI

with Jess Greenwood

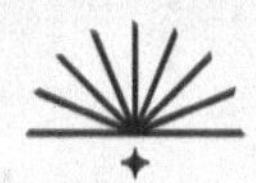

Published and distributed by Soul Speak Press

An imprint of Merack Publishing

Library of Congress Control Number:

ISBN: (eBook) 978-1-958472-42-2
ISBN: (paperback) 978-1-958472-41-5
ISBN: (hardcover) 978-1-958472-43-9

This work is nonfiction and, as such, reflects the author's memory of her experiences.

To my family and my girlfriends,
whose love and belief in me lit the way through darkness.
Because of you, I know I am never alone.
And to every survivor
who dares to shatter the silence—
May your truth bring healing, justice, and light.

Part I of this memoir includes descriptions of childhood sexual abuse, physical violence, and suicidal ideation, which some may find triggering. Please take care when reading.

PREFACE

Had you asked me five years ago what I'd be doing with my life in my sixties, I never would have said I'd be writing a memoir, revealing the deepest, darkest secret of my life, and publicly speaking about it to the world while still working full-time.

For most of my life, I vowed to keep my trauma a secret. And I did. For fifty years.

What I couldn't foresee was what would happen when the truth finally burst wide open, when those who abused me were confronted. I had believed that acknowledgement and an apology were all I needed—that with validation I could forgive and the burden would be lifted. Such a simple concept. But when the apology never came, I had to face the question: How do you heal when the words you long to hear never arrive?

That's when I decided to tell my story. At first, writing the memoir was for me. Putting my experience on these pages became incredibly cathartic. I was forced to relive memories I wanted to escape, but the process also uncovered new memories I had no idea existed as my brain continued to heal. Through this process, I found clarity.

There are moments in these pages where I don't come across in the best light. And I'm okay with that. Healing isn't neat or polished. It's messy. It's flawed. To see the good in me, you also have to see the brokenness—the pain I carried, the choices I made, and the ways I moved forward despite it all.

I was seven years old when the world first betrayed me.

Behind the quiet facade of an upper-middle-class suburban childhood, my life fractured in ways I couldn't understand. I will never know where the dark impulse to hurt came from and why my two oldest brothers chose to betray me, but I've learned that those questions—while once all consuming—no longer define me.

This memoir is not a catalog of the assaults I endured. While Part I includes some of those painful truths, this story is not about what *they did*. It's about what *I did* to survive.

Still, I know that reading the truth of someone else's trauma can be heavy. If at any point this story feels overwhelming, I invite you to pause, breathe, and return when you are ready. Healing doesn't follow a straight line, and neither does my story.

When I began this journey in late 2024, I still believed I was the only one this happened to. Ashamed. Embarrassed. Alone. But I've since discovered that I am not alone at all. I've met hundreds of other survivors, families, and advocates who are also speaking out, telling their stories, and shattering the silence. Sadly, I know I'll meet thousands more victims in my journey. My intent in writing this memoir was to finally give "Little Darlene" a voice. She deserves that. And so do the countless others who've endured sibling sexual trauma and abuse (SSTA)—or any form of abuse for that matter—in silence.

I've joined in their efforts, not only for my own healing, but to help others find theirs. Together we are breaking taboos. We are reclaiming our voices. I once said that if sharing my story helped even one other person, going public would be worth it. I still believe that.

This is not just a story of trauma. It's also a story of resilience. It's about holding on to the 90 percent of my life that was good, even while 10 percent was poisoned—and choosing not to let the darkness win.

So, while this book is written for survivors, it's also for anyone who has faced something that threatened to steal their joy, their purpose, their future, their voice. If you've ever wondered how to keep going when everything hurts—this book is for you.

I hope my journey helps you find your own strength.

I hope it reminds you that no matter what you've faced, you are never alone.

And I hope it inspires you to rise—again and again—until you create the life you were meant to live.

Author's Note

This is my story, told as I remember it. The experiences and memories you'll read here are true to my life. In most places, I've changed names to protect the individuals' privacy. In other places, I have not.

At the end of this book, I've also shared some resources—people, organizations, and practices—that supported me on my path. They made a difference for me, and maybe they'll be helpful for you too.

The DeLoy Family

Helen: Born 1927. Died 2021.

Gerald (Jerry): Born 1930. Died 2025.

Diane: Born 1955. Died 2008. 11 years older.

David: Born 1958. 8 years older.

Don: Born 1961. 5 years older.

Dale: Born 1963. 3 years older.

Darlene: Born 1966.

PART I

THE *ALMOST* PERFECT CHILDHOOD

1970s ERA DOG N SUDS.

1
CLARENCE, NEW YORK, 1973

Behind every strong woman is a story that gave her no other choice.
—NAKEIA HOMER

Stilts yelled back at me, "Come on, Darlene!" as she purposefully strode down the dusty road with her long, tan legs. She earned her nickname with those legs, and she could move fast when she wanted to.

Giggling at my own mischief, I did another cartwheel and jogged the rest of the way down the road to catch up with her. I was always doing cartwheels back then. There was just something intoxicating about feeling my legs fly through the air. If anyone ever came looking for me, my mom would shake her head with a smile and say, "Did you look for the girl doing cartwheels? That's my little gymnast, Darlene."

I remember how the summer sun warmed our shoulders as we walked side by side down to the end of Stilts' unpaved road where it intersected with Main Street. We turned right and kept going past the General Store to the Dog N Suds. While summers in upstate New York were generally pretty mild, it was hot enough that I was looking forward to a root beer in a frosted mug. At seven, I couldn't yet handle the full liter stein that came standard, but an ice-cold Junior Pint would do just fine. It was rare that our parents gave us money for lunch and allowed us to walk all the way down Main Street alone, so this was an extra special treat.

Stilts picked up the pace again, breaking free of my hand to run the last few steps to the window as I exclaimed, "Jeez Louise! Why are you running?!?" She was grinning as I made it to the window next to her.

"Because I need that root beer now, and you were going TOO SLOW!" She laughed, bumping me with her hip to let me know she was just messing with me.

The Dog N Suds was a classic drive-in, cars pulling into bays to order standard grill fare through the silver intercoms affixed to bright red poles outside the driver's side window. We'd watch, transfixed, as the car hops juggled plastic trays piled high with cheeseburgers, Coney dogs, fries, and shakes. When they got to the car with an order, they would deftly hook the tray on to the passenger side window, the back window, too, if the car held a family-full. What could be better than car-side service?

In our case, table-side service would have to do. There was nowhere to sit inside the Dog N Suds, so after we placed our order at the window, we made our way over to the old picnic tables under the bright red and yellow awning. They weren't anything special, utilitarian at best, but at that time of day, they offered a welcome break from the summer sun. While we waited for our food, we played with the Barbies we brought from home. Our constant companions, I recall dragging them with us everywhere, probably explaining why most of them were missing an arm or a leg. We'd pretend they were desperate for a root beer too and set them up tea-party style in anticipation of our meal.

When our orders were ready, the car hops would shuttle them over to our table, half annoyed, half amused at our elaborate tea party set up. Besides the root beer, our standard order was a Coney dog and french fries. It is absolute sacrilege to disgrace a Coney dog with ketchup. We'd douse the dog with mustard instead, and Stilts would add onions (Yuck!). Once they were ready, we'd lock eyes, and collectively take the biggest bite possible, globs of gooey mustard oozing out of the bun and covering our faces and hands. The ketchup we saved exclusively for our fries. Squirting an overly generous portion into our red-and-white trays, we'd dissolve into giggles when the bottle made rude noises. Once our bellies were full of Coney dog, we could be more generous with the fries. Taking a tiny nibble, we'd pass a crisp fry over to Barbie for an imaginary bite. Back and forth. Back and forth. Needless to say, the tea party took awhile.

After everyone had their fair share, we wiped our faces and hands with napkins from the dispenser. It looked like a massacre had taken place after we cleaned up all of the condiments. We smiled somewhat apologetically at the people working the window as we dumped our trays and mountains of red-and-yellow smudged napkins into the trash bins.

On our way back to Stilts' house, we popped into the General Store. Bins of candy sticks teased us, but it was the ice cream we came for. Something cool to keep us company on the long walk back. Rocky road for Stilts and mint chocolate chip for me. It's been my favorite flavor all my life.

That was summer in 1973. Me and Stilts. The Dog N Suds. Cartwheels, Coney dogs, and ice cream.

It may sound odd that two little girls were allowed to walk to the local hamburger joint alone at the young age of seven, but in 1973 in Clarence, New York, and, frankly, in most of America, that was entirely normal. As the youngest of five children—Diane, David, Don, Dale, and me—I was used to loose parental oversight. Like most big families back then, my mom was a verifiable taxi, always busy driving one of us to a practice here or a Scouts meeting there. Diane had her driver's license, but she was working that summer saving for college and wasn't around much. Stilts had three brothers herself, similar in age to mine, and her father had a big-time job as a commentator for the nearby professional sports team. He was working most of the time, and her mom was doing the same thing as mine. So, all of us kids entertained ourselves.

And there was a lot to keep us busy.

Stilts' family lived in a sprawling three-story white house that sat on the top of a big hill. It was the most beautiful house I had ever seen. The front yard dropped down to an old rock quarry that marked the halfway point of their property. The quarry had been filled by a freshwater spring years ago, so it was a wonderful, albeit freezing, watering hole for us kids. Despite the cold, we swam in that thing almost every day. Stilts' family trucked in sand to create a small beach area and built a long dock with a diving board and a big blue slide off the ends. The water was dark and murky, and I was frankly terrified to swim in it. Having only previously swam in crystal clear swimming pools, my imagination went wild when I thought about all of the creatures that could be down there. It didn't help that one day while out in the row boat, Stilts' dad pointed out a black snake slithering around the edge of the water. Talk about freaking a little girl out!

My dad took notice that I was scared of the quarry. Knowing that I was likely to spend a lot of time in the water with Stilts that summer, he wanted to make sure I could swim safely. At the time, I was still wearing a life jacket when I went off the slide or jumped off the dock. One day, Dad stood on the dock and watched me swim. After a while, he pulled me up and said gently, "Honey, I think you've had enough practice with the life jacket and you know how to swim. Let's just get you going."

I don't recall him being aggressive about it; he wasn't threatening me, more warming me up to the idea. We stood at the end of the dock while he gave me instructions. First, he threw me in with the life jacket on, and I was to swim by myself back to the dock. He did that a couple of times, each time throwing me further and further out. Finally, he was satisfied and said, "You're ready. Let's do this!"

I was so happy to have my father's attention that I forgot this game was leading to something, so my little girl nerves kicked in hard when we took the life jacket off for good. Dad threw me out pretty far and I started to sink. At first, I was just relieved my feet hadn't found a critter as the image of that big, black snake loomed large in my mind. But then I realized I was under water, and I had to get up! I kicked my legs and pushed the water away with my arms like I'd been taught. It felt like it took forever. I started to panic that I wasn't going to make it in time, the air burning in my lungs as I kept kicking. I came up sputtering, heart pounding, but the look on my dad's face was all I needed to proudly doggie paddle back to the dock. Dad looked down at me with a smirk on his face. "Told you you could swim," he said.

I cherished these moments with my father. He was a quiet man with little tolerance for small talk. His focus was on his work, climbing the corporate ladder to support his family. Additionally, as with most men of his era, his respect and, by default, his attention, went to the boys in the family. It was rare for me to get his undivided attention. Earning his approval that day, and even more so, being able to make him proud, meant everything to me.

*　　*　　*

When we weren't swimming in the quarry, we were fishing in it with my next oldest brother Dale and Stilts' brothers. I mostly liked to watch while everyone fished, but every now and then I would try my hand at it. Most of the time, I could put the worm on the hook on my own, but those things were slippery little critters and sometimes they got away from me. I'd scramble around the dock to grab them whenever I'd drop one, the boys chuckling at my butterfingers. Eventually, I learned the trick. Take one end and stick the hook in it. Then, keep twisting and twisting until you get a hold of the other end and stick that in the hook. Voila! Ready to cast!

It took a lot of practice to get enough leverage to cast the line on our old-school bamboo poles. Short cast? Reel it back in. Flat or loose cast with too much line? Reel it back in. But finally I could manage a solid cast, sending it out just far enough that there was some tension on the line. I watched patiently, waiting to see the telltale sign of the bobber going up and down. When it started to move, one of us would yell, "Fish! Fish! You got one!" It was so exciting to feel that jerk on the pole. *Reel it in slowly—but not too slowly. Come on. Come on. Bring it in.* One of the boys would stand next to me with the net, ready to scoop up the fish as soon as it popped out of the water. Finally, the hook would crest the water and a little sunfish or bluegill would flap wildly from the end of the line. A round of cheers would go up from the dock. "Got one!" I'd yell.

There was only one problem. I hated taking the fish off the hook. No matter how many times I tried, I just couldn't do it. It was hard for me to grab hold of the fish because I was so afraid of their spiny back fins! I would push the spiny fin flat with one hand while I tried to get the hook out of its mouth with the other, but sometimes the hook was in so deep, I just couldn't manage to maneuver it out on my own. Frustration would take over and finally I'd give up, pleading with one of the boys to help me. For a while they would just rip the hook out and hand me back my fish so we could add it to our daily tally. But as the day wore on, they'd realize who was doing all the work. I could usually sweet talk Dale into helping the longest, but eventually he'd shoot back, "You haven't gotten a single fish off a hook all day! Now it's your turn." A little salty but not one for quitting, I'd prepare my rod to cast again, determined to remove the hook myself the next time.

We'd spend all day like this, swimming, fishing, paddling. When the sun started to fade, Stilts and I would trudge up to their wooden changing house halfway up the hill to swap our wet clothes for dry ones. That was one of the only firm rules in Stilts' house—no wet clothes! Once we'd changed, we'd race up the rest of the hill to the main house. The family room might as well have been our stage. We'd crowd around their record player, picking out vinyls from the heartthrobs of the day—Shaun Cassidy, Leif Garrett, and our favorite, Donny Osmond. Once we dropped that needle and the vinyl started turning, the show was on. Singing and dancing, our school girl crushes came to life as we belted out the lyrics to "Puppy Love"—no one understood us like Donny. We just knew he was singing directly to us.

*   *   *

In Clarence, we lived in the Brady Bunch house. At least, that's what the outside looked like to me. A typical 1970s split-level, the main floor housed the shared living space in a sort of merry-go-round layout with all of the rooms forming a semicircle around one big wall in the middle. Out of the kitchen there was a half set of stairs that led to the bedrooms. I always thought there were six stairs, not because I counted, but because I remember thinking someone cut a full set of stairs in half and left us with the other half.

At the top of the stairs on the right was the kids' bathroom, a long, hall-like dungeon that all five of us shared until Diane mercifully left for college. Of course, that meant I shared a bathroom with three boys, so it was pretty disgusting most of the time. David had the first bedroom across the hall from the bathroom. He'd recently graduated to having his own room once Diane moved out. It was a point of pride for him as the oldest boy, especially since Don and Dale were still sharing the "boys room" at the very end of the hallway. His bedroom reflected the typical Draconian darkness of a sixteen-year-old teenage boy, lava lamps and all. Mom picked out this red chenille bedspread with a tufted flower pattern trying to lighten up the room, except it was oddly complementary with the black walls and mood lighting. I'll never forget the Braille-like feeling of that bedspread's pattern underneath my fingers.

Next to David's room was my bedroom. As the baby, and the only girl left following a long line of boys, I always got my own room. I didn't realize what a luxury that was until much later.

That particular morning, I was in my room rushing to change into my bathing suit so I could go meet Stilts and her brothers down at the quarry. We had made a plan the day before to go fishing. After chowing down some breakfast, I was eager to head that way.

The house was quiet, not unusual on a summer morning as Dad went into the office early and Mom was taking Dale and Don to base-ball practice. I had seen her earlier as she hurried out the door with the older boys and relayed my plan for the day. "Just make sure you're home by dark, Darlene," she said as she grabbed her purse and keys.

Changed and ready to go, I walked out of my room into the hallway, on my way to the stairs, when David popped his head out of his own bedroom and said, "Darlene, come here. I want to show you something."

"What is it?" I asked, slightly annoyed that he was delaying my progress, but never wanting to miss out on anything exciting my older brothers were willing to show me.

He insisted, "I've got something really cool to show you. Just come here."

I followed him into his bedroom, standing just inside the door at the end of his massive bed. The red bedspread was all disheveled as

David never made his bed. I remember being exasperated that he was so sloppy. I always made my bed.

He reached around me and shut the door.

And then he locked it.

I heard the lock turn. Subconsciously, I registered the sound, how odd it was to lock the door, but I didn't question it. I was focused on what he was going to show me, silently willing him to hurry up so I wouldn't be late to meet Stilts.

He walked around me, talking fast: "Oh my God, Darlene, you'll never believe what I want to show you." An unfamiliar sound. His belt. The metal of the buckle jangling against the button on his pants as he undid it. The swish of the black leather coming through the belt loops. I remember seeing his bare ass as his pants dropped to his ankles. Confusion. We did not live in a house where we got naked in front of each other. *Why would he pull down his pants with me in the room?*

David sat back down on the bed, now fully exposed, and said, "Come here."

I yelled, "What are you doing? Why are you doing this?" whipping around to get out of the room. David grabbed my arm before I could make contact with the doorknob. "No, Darlene, you have to stay. You have to take care of me."

He pulled me down onto the edge of his bed and used the weight of his body to hold me there. At a mere fifty pounds, I felt like I was suffocating under the bulk of his sixteen-year-old body. I tried again to get free, or at least, I think I did, the red flowers on the bedspread rough against my fingers as I grabbed for something to pull me away. He started to touch himself down there, down in places I wasn't supposed to see. I watched his elbow move back and forth, slowly at first and then faster and faster. He grunted, and I levitated. Time and space fell away as I felt myself float out of my trapped body. I could see myself from above, him partially on top of me, my tiny body with its soul still struggling to get out that door.

In the future, people will ask "Did you scream? Did you fight?" Every day after, I asked myself, "Could I have screamed louder? Fought harder?" But I don't think these are the right questions. Even if I had screamed my loudest scream or fought my hardest fight, who would have helped me? The house was empty, and David knew it.

He leaned over me, hot breath landing on my ear so the words were quiet, but unmistakable: "Don't you ever say a word, Darlene. This is something just between us. This is what brothers and sisters do. If you ever tell Mom and Dad, I'll tell them you're a liar. No one will believe you. They will kick you out, and you will be an orphan."

I don't know what happened next, but I know I believed him.

It is estimated that sibling sexual assault (SSA) may be up to three times as common as sexual abuse by a parent or caregiver.[1]

* * *

While we were in Clarence, my mom started working as a real estate agent. I don't know if we needed the money or she just wanted an excuse to get out of the house. Life was already hectic enough with four active kids, each with their own schedule of Scout meetings, practices, and games to manage. I remember that our house was

---

1   Peter Yates and Stuart Allardyce, *Sibling Sexual Abuse: A Knowledge and Practice Overview* (Centre of Expertise on Child Sexual Abuse, 2021), https://www.csacentre.org.uk/app/uploads/2023/09/Sibling-sexual-abuse-report.pdf.

always a disaster. We ran out of toilet paper at times and never had basic things like napkins. If you wanted your laundry done, you did it yourself. Dinner was usually a fend-for-yourself situation. Mom tried, but she was a horrible cook, and we never had time to sit down together anyway. Not exactly the ideal household. It was part of the reason we never had friends over. We were embarrassed.

That's not to say Mom wasn't loving or attentive. She was. But largely in things that took place outside our home. She was incredibly involved in the community and our extracurricular activities. She served as my Brownie leader and volunteered at our school, doing the things "good moms" do. Appearances mattered to Mom. She was always more concerned with what was happening outside our home than in it.

Thinking about it now, I don't believe she ever wanted to be a stay-at-home mom. She was the first one in her family to go to college and didn't marry until twenty-seven, a regular "Old Maid" by those days' standards. I wonder if she had ambitions and dreams I never knew about, a whole life that just couldn't exist in the same space as the five of us kids.

Eventually, we left Clarence as my dad pursued his own ambitions. He was offered an incredible job as the senior vice president of engineering at Mueller Brass in Port Huron, Michigan. His efforts to climb the corporate ladder were working. While we were never poor, this new job came with perks we were not used to at the time—a corner office, a company car, and a private country club membership. The prospect of this new lifestyle made the idea of moving more palatable, exciting even.

We were planning to move over the summer, so at the end of the school year, Mom allowed me to throw a going-away party. I felt so adult. I handwrote twelve invitations and ceremoniously handed them out to all of my friends. Stilts, of course, but also girls from school and Brownies and our neighborhood. I felt so lucky to have that many friends that wanted to say goodbye to me.

On the day of the big event, Mom took all of us to the park for a picnic lunch. We played tag and kickball and hung upside down on the monkey bars. Feet in the air, I lifted my head for a second to stare at the sky. *This is what perfect feels like,* I thought.

After exhausting ourselves at the park, we took a break to rest and regroup but the day wasn't over. That night, all of the girls came over to our house. Looking back, it was one of the only times I can remember having friends at my house. Maybe that's part of the reason I was so excited. We hijacked the lower-level den, sleeping bags and stuffed animals strewn all over that rust-colored shag carpet. Already in pajamas, most of us were ready to start the festivities. Slumber parties with little girls then are much like slumber parties with little girls now, and so it wasn't long before one of us started chanting, "Light as a feather, stiff as a board. Light as a feather, stiff as a board."

We kneeled in a circle of trust for more than an hour, surrounding the willing participant laying prone on the floor. With two fingers from each little hand under her back, we were fully convinced that she would lift spontaneously off the floor in raptured levitation. It didn't happen. So when we finally got tired and Mom started yelling for us to be quiet and go to bed, we began to set out the sleeping bags intending to just pretend we were going to sleep.

Eventually, some of my friends started nodding off, leaving themselves vulnerable to the hallmark of sleepovers . . . prank time. We snuck up the half set of stairs to the kitchen and filled two bowls with water, one hot and one cold. Smothering our giggles, we tiptoed back downstairs to put the hands of one sleeping beauty into the different water bowls. With rapt anticipation, we waited to see whether she'd pee herself in her sleeping bag. While we were waiting, we snagged the bag of chips we'd been munching on all night and sprinkled the crumbs inside the covers of another sleeping friend. It was supposed to make her itch in her sleep. Or so we'd heard. None of these pranks ever worked, but that wasn't really the point. The feeling of camaraderie, shared secrets, and love flooded through me. I was not alone. All of my friends were here with me.

The few of us that made it past midnight finally got sleepy enough to wriggle into our own bags, occasional giggles still bursting out as we thought about the night's antics. In the morning, you might imagine that the subjects of our pranks were at least a bit annoyed, but truth be told, they weren't. And if there had been any hurt feelings, my mother's custom pancakes, made into any shape or letter the girls wanted, smoothed things over.

I was so focused on the fun, so caught up in the presents and the flattery, the perceived safety of a life filled with friends, that I don't actually remember being sad about leaving Clarence. Or maybe there was just something there I was ready to leave behind, hoping that it wouldn't follow me.

*   *   *

Mom wanted to take her time finding the perfect house for our family in Port Huron, but Dad needed to begin work, so they rented a trailer for the summer. A big, white rectangle, it sat right on the beach. It wasn't in a trailer park, or inside a community. In fact, it wasn't really anywhere. It looked like it had washed up straight out of Lake Huron, settling on the beach just past where the water could pull it back into the deep.

My dad lived there during the week and would come back and forth to Clarence on the weekends. We kids largely stayed in Clarence for the summer, not wanting to miss our respective sports practices, so we only spent one week at the trailer for what our parents dubbed a "vacation." I didn't like the trailer. It was too cramped for our big family, not enough bedrooms, only one bathroom, and nothing that felt like ours. All of the surfaces were white—white cupboards, white counters, white tile. The whole place felt sterile, like living in a hospital, not a home.

The one redeeming factor was the proximity of the trailer to the lake. Dale and I took advantage of this prime location, spending hours on the beach with our buckets and shovels. We constructed elaborate sand castles. Turrets and balustrades and walls dotted with original shell decorations. Each castle had to have a moat, to protect the inhabitants, of course. After we dug and dug, creating deep troughs around the four sides of our castle, we'd carry buckets of water from the lake to fill it up, our legs straining with the effort. Eventually, we realized if we built the castle closer to the lake, we wouldn't have to walk as far. Our crowning achievement was learning how to place the castle just close enough that the waves would push water into the moat without us having to do a thing.

Between castle building and bucket carrying, we'd bury each other in the sand, meticulously covering every inch of our exposed skin. I had turned eight that January, and while I was still a scrawny little thing, it took Dale a solid hour to cover me completely. I liked to mess with him, so once he'd finished my legs and moved on to my arms, I'd wiggle my toes, setting them free from the sand. He wouldn't notice until he stood up to take in his masterpiece. His satisfied smile sliding as he saw the offensive toes poking through, he would yell with exasperation, "Dang it, Darlene! Stay still!" I'd feign innocence and go back to pretending to be a mummy, but it never lasted very long.

I was always with Dale when we were at the trailer, except on this particular day. I don't know where Dale was, maybe on the beach waiting for me, maybe not. But I found myself alone in the cramped trailer with David. I walked out of the lone bathroom, its door adjacent to the door to my parents' bedroom, the big one at the back. David grabbed my wrist, "Hey, come here."

There was no fake excitement this time. His tone was forceful, ominous almost. He yanked me into the bedroom, pulled the door shut, and locked it behind him.

"This time, you're going to take care of me," he said, determination in his eyes. "This time we're going to do it right." His hand was still wound around my wrist, pulling me closer and closer to the bed.

"If you leave this room, Darlene, I'm going to kill you. You are not leaving this room." Fear crawled up my spine as tears spilled from my eyes.

"Stop, David, please stop." I started to shake, his left hand still firmly around my wrist as his right hand undid his belt buckle. The same black belt, the big gold buckle clanking against the button as he pulled it free from his pants.

"This is what we're going to do. I'm going to lay down on the bed, and you're going to whip me with my belt. Don't hold it by the buckle, hold it by the end, see?" He let go of my wrist to take his pants off, intent on showing me exactly what he wanted done. He laid down on the bed on his belly, butt cheeks exposed, waiting for me to comply.

"Okay, Darlene, do it!" he said. Horrified, I lifted my arm in the air and tentatively brought the end of the belt down on his bare buttocks. In that split second, I felt a small portal between hell and freedom open. He was face down, pants down, and I had a chance.

Dropping the belt, I turned, whipping the door knob to the left to release the pop lock. I threw my body through the opening, slamming the door behind me to buy a few precious seconds. I tore down the hallway, focused only on getting out of that trailer. I made it to the front door and tried the knob, rattling it with my trembling hands as I heard David yelling my name behind me, struggling to get his pants back on. I don't know why I couldn't get the door open. Maybe fear paralyzed my fingers. Stuck, I turned, panicked, knowing I needed to find a place to hide. I spotted the laundry room at the end of the hall closest to the living room and scooted in, eyeing the tall cupboard where we kept the broom and the mop. I squeezed my tiny body in between the handles, closing the cupboard door behind me as silently as possible. I tried to slow my breathing, still my heart as I heard David crashing down the hall after me. I would be safe if I could just. keep. quiet.

The cupboard door flew open, David's eyes, now bright with anger.

He yanked me out by my arm, breathing hard now, spittle flying from his lips as he yelled, "You are going to do this, Darlene." He dragged me into the hallway, pulling me back toward the bedroom, my kicking and fighting no match for his strength. I kept slapping my free arm against the walls, trying to find something to grab on to, anything in that long, dark, sterile hallway to help me hold on. There was nothing. He finally got me back into the bedroom and threw me on the bed. I landed hard. I heard the door shut behind him. And then that sound. The one that proved the portal was permanently closed; there was no escape from hell.

The lock.

It's the last thing I remember.

Signs of inappropriate sexual contact between siblings include contact that occurs with coercion, intimidation, or force.[2]

---

2   Yates and Allardyce, *Sibling Sexual Abuse* (2021).

ME IN MY FAVORITE FIGURE SKATING OUTFIT.

1975, PORT HURON, MICHIGAN. OUR BLUE SALTBOX HOUSE.

2

PORT HURON, MICHIGAN, 1974

The saddest thing about betrayal is that it never comes from your enemies;
it comes from those you trust the most.

—UNKNOWN

Betrayal is such a big word for an eight-year-old. How could someone so young experience something so big, so . . . dramatic?

But that's what I felt. Betrayed.

I thought the world operated with clear rules and roles. Brothers, especially older brothers, were supposed to be protectors. They existed in large part to keep their sisters, especially their younger sisters, safe from the dangers of the world. They weren't supposed to *be* the danger.

Except, now danger existed in my own home. Steps from my bedroom. At the dinner table. In our basement. Our new home in

Port Huron was supposed to be a fresh start, and maybe it could be, would be, but I had no way of knowing whether or not the past would follow me there.

Fear is a funny thing. It seeps out of dark corners and from behind tree branches, manifesting in an anxiety that was far more pervasive than I realized even then. I consciously knew that the only person who had hurt me was David, but after his assaults, the fear became bigger than just him. It was a constant presence, my reluctant companion. If the very person meant to protect me could so egregiously violate that role, how could I trust that I was safe anywhere? Or with anyone?

The fear started to leak out, finding ways to nip at my subconscious until I gave it the attention it sought. I could keep it at bay during the day, when I was with other people, or focused on one of my activities, but as night fell, the fear would creep back in. Walking back from a friend's house at dusk, I could feel the panic rising in my chest as the sun dripped down the horizon. The hair on the back of my neck rose as I perceived shadows with predatory eyes peering out from the trees, stalking my every move, about to attack me at any second. The darker it got, the faster my legs moved, until I was literally running toward the relative safety of our door. I would pause in the breezeway of that beautiful blue saltbox house, the one that looked like everything and everyone inside was perfect. Heaving and shaking, I would try to slow my breathing before walking in the door. As I entered the family room, Mom would look up, take in my disheveled state, breath still coming short and fast and say, "Darlene, why are you so out of breath?"

I can't tell you how many times I lied, dismissing her concern by saying something slightly ridiculous like "I just like running." That explanation seemed to be good enough for her, as she was always distracted, busy trying to get some sort of dinner on the table. I assume she figured me being home on time was good enough.

To this day, I hate running.

*   *   *

The new house may not have gotten rid of my fear, but it did offer its own kind of opportunity. Dad's new job afforded Mom the ability to pick a home in a more upscale neighborhood. Our street held fourteen houses, each on a spacious lot, with mature trees in the yards and woods serving as the back property line. Like our family, every neighbor on our street had at least three to four kids, so there were plenty of potential friends around.

I can't say that I did it consciously at the time. I doubt eight-year-olds craft such strategic plans, but some part of me must have calculated that if being at home meant I was at risk, protecting myself meant never being at home. And the way to ensure I was out of the house from dawn to dusk was to make friends. Lots of them. More friends meant more invites. And more invites meant less opportunity for David to come after me.

We moved to Port Huron in the summer of 1974, and I got right to work making friends in the neighborhood. I knew I was short on time to build those relationships before school started, so I studied the map of the neighbors' houses given to us by the Neighborhood Welcome Committee, each house marked with the number, age, and gender of the kids that lived there. I starred the houses that seemed promising and would go down to introduce myself. One of the easiest conversation starters was school since we all went to the same one.

The neighborhood crew was adamant that I wanted Mrs. Kish for third grade, *not* Mrs. Bush. I begged my mom to ask the principal if I could have Mrs. Kish. When we went to register me for school, Mom did ask that I be assigned to Mrs. Kish's classroom, but the principal turned her attention to me. I sat there, desperately trying to think of an appropriate answer to her inquiries about why I wanted to be in Mrs. Kish's classroom so badly. Of course, of all the injustices, the first day of third grade, I walked into my new school only to find myself assigned to Mrs. Bush's classroom. I stewed all day long, and when school finally let out, I raced home to share my righteous rage with my new friends.

It was important to me that these kids liked me. If they thought Mrs. Bush was mean, I did too. And if I couldn't get my mom to fix the situation, then at least I could use the unfairness of it all to garner sympathy in the neighborhood. I maybe played it up a little more than necessary, but the acceptance, and, even more so, the solidarity I felt with the kids on the street was totally worth it.

Legitimately, third grade proved to be more difficult than second. Whether Port Huron schools were more advanced than the schools in Clarence or whether I was just distracted by too many things, I don't know, but I had to work harder there to be an overachiever. This became increasingly more difficult when I started getting pulled out for speech therapy. I couldn't get my mouth to form the sounds for "sh" and "ch" correctly. The word *church* was particularly frustrating with its double "ch," so I largely tried to avoid it, which was hard to do when we started going every week. I remember being bothered not just by my difficulty with compound consonants, but more so by the embarrassment of being pulled out for extra help. Here I was, new kid in a new school, with the meanest teacher, already being singled out.

All of these things were working against me. I wanted to be popular. I *needed* to be popular.

It wasn't just about kids liking me, although, of course, that was nice. Being popular became my safety net, my security blanket. I wanted to build a wall of people around me.

* * *

Kenzi and her family lived down the street from us, and she and I became fast friends, bonding over a shared love of *The Sound of Music*. Normally, we were outside all of the time, but when the weather didn't allow it, we were in Kenzi's basement. Down there, we became directors and producers, staging our own reenactment of the classic story. Kenzi's mom owned the entire score on vinyl, so all of the neighborhood kids would gather around the record player and belt out spirited renditions of "Do-Re-Mi." The girls always quibbled over who was going to be Liesl, so before singing "Sixteen Going on Seventeen," we had to assign parts. We mainly did this through the highly sophisticated method of drawing straws. It was easy with the boy parts since we often didn't have any boys join us except Kenzi's younger brother, and he never minded stepping into the role of the handsome Rolf. Secretly, I always wanted to play Gretl. She had such a spirited temperament, but she was doted on by her brothers and sisters, and as the baby of my own family, it just seemed fitting.

After months of practicing the entire score in the basement by ourselves, we finally got the idea to hold an actual production for our parents. For this one special show, I successfully won the part of Gretl. When the time came for "So Long, Farewell," it almost felt like we were actually in the movie. The stairs in Kenzi's basement were the perfect place to reenact the memorable scene, and with the parents waving from their makeshift theater seats below, it felt almost real. When it was time for little Gretl to issue the final farewell, I put my all into the lyrics, faking a yawn and saying goodnight to the sun. When my stage sister Liesl came to carry me up the stairs, I let my weight fall into her arms, soaking in the feeling of safety and love.

I so desperately wanted to live in Gretl's story instead of my own. The stairs in her home led to brothers and sisters who loved and protected her. The steps in my home led to my abuser.

*   *   *

Despite the fear, I loved Port Huron. As third grade progressed, I got used to Mrs. Bush (she wasn't actually that mean), and speech therapy became just a normal part of my week. I succeeded in being popular, at least by my own definition, and I accepted every invitation to every birthday party, sleepover, and playdate. As we said back then, my social card was full.

There were still times when my new friends were otherwise occupied which left me with down time I didn't want. My brothers Dale and Don were always out of the house playing sports. Their practices and games consumed their daylight and evening hours, and I would often see them come home late just to cram in some food, do a little homework, and crash. I craved that level of busy.

So in the winter of my third grade year, I started figure skating. I'm not sure I could have convinced Mom to make the thirty minute drive to the rink multiple times a week if it was all on her, but what sold her on the idea was sharing carpooling duties with the new neighbor girl's mom. When she moved in across the street, the two of us signed up for the same lessons. We may have started the season looking like awkward ducks, arms held out to keep us from falling, but by the end of winter we were expertly gliding forward and backward and had even started learning the figure eight. I gravitated toward the freedom of figure skating, and once I mastered the art of spotting so I didn't get dizzy during the spins, that feeling of whipping around on the ice became intoxicating.

I was inspired by Dorothy Hamill, also a Midwestern girl, who began her figure skating career at age eight as well. By 1975, she was working her way to the Olympic gold medal and her signature look was popular in the media. I became obsessed with her haircut, the famous bob known as the "short and sassy" and begged my mother to cut my hair just like hers. Mom was adamantly against it at first. I don't think she wanted her church friends mistaking her little girl for a boy. But eventually the pleading worked, my long brunette locks falling to the floor as she muttered under her breath with each snip.

I don't think she expected me to like it; but I did. I didn't look like a girl anymore. And if I didn't look like a girl, why would a boy, any boy, want me to touch them?

My interest in sports didn't stop with figure skating. I wasn't putting in thirty hours of practice a week like Dorothy, so I had time to add other interests. I started gymnastics about this time and as the weather got warmer, I picked up girls hardball too. I may have been labeled a tomboy with my short hair and athletic activities, but I wasn't trying to be. I was just intent on being the opposite of whatever it was that made girls interesting to boys.

*　*　*

Before having kids, my mother was a second grade teacher. Naturally creative, she had a knack for thinking up activities for her students that would introduce them to art and nature. She loved being a teacher. The first one in her family to go to college, she was proud of being able to hold such a professional job. In the 1950s, though, you weren't allowed to teach while pregnant. So six months into her pregnancy with Diane, when she could no longer hide it, she was forced to resign. It saddens me that Mom was denied the opportunity to pursue a career she clearly treasured. I imagine that experience had a significant impact on her self-esteem, her identity. Society expected her to be a homemaker. And that was that. There was no room or tolerance for what she wanted. I wonder if that incredibly unfair tradeoff explains why she didn't try very hard to keep our home up. That wasn't a role she had chosen for herself.

While she may not have been the best housekeeper, Mom passed on her creative spirit to all of us kids. With the woods and the lake close by, our neighborhood was the perfect classroom. On any given Saturday when the weather was nice, Mom might look out the window and declare, "Let's go for a walk!"

Mom and I would go tromping around in the woods, her gently encouraging me to take my time, to look with curious eyes at the world around us. When we came across a bird, we'd quickly cross reference its coloring and beak with the pictures in one of my bird books. Mom always had me bring a bag on these treks and instructed me to collect as many different leaves and bark as possible so we could research what type of tree they came from. We would then flatten and dry the leaves between pieces of wax paper and secure them in one of the homemade scrapbooks Mom put together for me. After identifying the correct tree, she would help me draw what the tree looked like next to each leaf.

In Michigan, the sassafras tree is a beloved species because its leaves often grow to look like a physical representation of the state itself. A thumb of sorts sticks out of the end of the leaf. Holding the leaves up to our own palms, we would mimic a common practice of Michigan residents who use their hand to visually explain where their particular city is located; Port Huron is on the outside edge of the thumb right at the bottom knuckle.

It is also a well known practice to make tea from parts of the sassafras tree. While the most common method is to strip the bark from the roots of the tree where the sap concentrates in the winter, it is also possible to make tea from the leaves and stems. In late summer before the chill of fall sets in, Mom would take me out to the woods with a more pointed purpose. She carried with her a small knife that she would use to separate long stems from the sassafras tree, the leaves creating a canopy so big I could almost hide under. Together, we'd carry the stems home and then carefully remove all of the leaves. Using the same knife, Mom would shave a fine outer layer off the stems. The stems would then steep in hot water for ten minutes or so, long enough to allow the deep brownish-red liquid to drip through the strainer into our cups to make the sassafras tea. Wrapping my little hands around a full mug, I would wait for Mom to add a touch of honey and then take a slow sip, careful not to burn my tongue. When it fully cooled, we would put the rest in the refrigerator to make iced tea for the next day. Perfect!

I remember the tea being delicious but it was the warmth of those moments with my mom that heated me from the inside. Her physical affection and undivided attention during these woodland walks were a temporary salve from the fear and betrayal, and a reminder of how important the rest of my family was to me.

*   *   *

Because we all went to the same school, lots of the kids that lived in and around the neighborhood also ended up being school friends. Freckles was both. Her house felt like a part of our neighborhood because I went there so often, but it really wasn't. To get to her house, you had to go down the wooded path, walk through the elementary school parking lot, across Lakeshore Road, and go all the way down her street to the very end. Freckles lived right on Lake Huron, so the half-mile walk was worth it, especially during the summer. I spent almost every day at her house the summer after third grade.

We weren't rebels by any means, but we had a lot of time on our hands and craved adventure. We started burning things in the woods right along the lake shore, tucked up by the trees so no one could see us, but not so close that we would catch anything on fire. While neither of our parents' smoked, it was commonplace to collect matches from all of the restaurants and bars in town, so we both had huge glass containers of matches sitting in our kitchens. We'd swipe a pack of matches and bring them down to the lake to burn whatever random item we could find. I have a permanent reminder of this game, the scar on my leg—proof that the pink plastic around a hair curler feels like molten lava when it touches your skin after being lit on fire.

Even though our parents weren't smokers, we were enthralled by the thin, blonde bombshells in all the '70s movies that were always lighting up long, white cigarettes, releasing a wispy trail of smoke from their pursed lips. We wanted to be just like them! Hershey and other candy confectioners took advantage of these desires, making candy cigarettes complete with sugar smoke that were sold in every candy store. Those were fun, but Freckles had other ideas for something a bit more original. Walking along the lakeshore, we would pick up driftwood left on the sand. Pulling long strips from the wood, we would light one with our swiped matches. I was terrified we would get caught, but Freckles would take a long drag, a mischievous grin spreading across her face as she fought back a cough. She'd puff out, "Take a chill pill, Darlene."

While I wasn't great at being naughty, I loved that feeling. The feeling of belonging. Of having a shared secret . . . one I actually wanted to keep.

Freckles and I were daring in other ways that summer too. When *Jaws* premiered in June 1975, it was the only thing the kids in the neighborhood could talk about. Being that Port Huron was on the water, even though it was lake water, it felt like this new summer blockbuster was about our town. Everyone was intent on going on opening day. On the younger end of the neighborhood crew, we had no idea what the movie was about; we were just happy to be included.

The Huron Theater was a downtown staple, and they went all out for the premier, constructing a huge paper-mache shark on the marquee. After waiting in line for what felt like hours, we finally made it into the theater. Immediately, my nose was assaulted by one of my most favorite smells in the world . . . movie theater popcorn. The butter. The salt. The crunch . . . my mouth waters just thinking about it. Freckles and I got a giant popcorn slathered in salt and butter and a jumbo Coke to split. Since the movie was rated PG, we didn't have to sneak in, but we felt like we were getting away with something as nine-year-olds when we took our seats in the packed theater. Thick, red velvet curtains buffeted the large projector screen which was a lot closer than I expected.

Real close.

Like third row close.

I remember sitting down and using my toes to scooch my butt back in my seat. Feet coming off the floor as I sat back, arms wrapped protectively around our giant bag of popcorn, I raised my eyes to the massive screen. Fear tickled my insides, but a different kind than I was used to. This fear was paired with another feeling . . . excitement. I turned my head to look at Freckles, bouncing in her seat with nervous energy. We grabbed hands as the lights went down, and I'm sure glad we did because I about died right there in my seat during the opening scene of the movie. For years after, I couldn't swim after dark. Even in lake water that I knew posed no threat. No way was I going down with the sharks.

* * *

By the fall of 1975 when I started fourth grade, some of my anxiety had eased. I had built a strong friend network both in my neighborhood and at school. Figure skating, gymnastics, and hardball kept me busy and out of the house, and sporting my tomboy bob, I felt less conspicuous, less likely to draw the attention of a boy, or my brother. Time was also creating a false sense of security, especially as we passed the year mark since the last assault. David was now seventeen, much more into partying, getting drunk, and smoking pot with his friends than being around us. We rarely saw each other; whether that was his disinterest in our family or my success at staying away from him, I don't know. And while I didn't feel safe, at least I didn't feel actively stalked. I started to hope that maybe this phase of my life was truly behind me. That it was "over."

But hope hurts that way. It weakens your resolve and makes you vulnerable to dangers you can't yet see.

My beautiful oak tree: My refuge.
My safety. My friend.

3

PORT HURON, MICHIGAN, 1975

You have no idea what it's like to be alone and scared when you're that little, and you know nobody's coming to save you.
—LUCY FROM *THE WISHING GAME*

Saturday nights were family time. When all of the work was done, all of the games played and practices attended, whoever was around would pile into the family room downstairs to watch a comedy show on TV. There were no televisions upstairs, so if you wanted to watch, you had to watch together. My dad would take up residence in his oversized blue chair, the leather kind with the buttons and the matching stool. The chair was actually an heirloom, passed down from my dad's father to him. Pushing your spine up against the tufted back felt like sitting inside of a hug. All of us kids raced to call dibs on the chair when Dad wasn't home, but on Saturday nights, that was Dad's chair . . . period. So, Mom and whoever else was home claimed spots on the gray-and-black tweed sectional, tucked our feet up underneath us, and got ready for the Saturday night lineup.

My parents loved to watch the comedy shows, particularly *The Carol Burnett Show* and *The Smothers Brothers Comedy Hour*. Variety shows like these were popular at the time, and in the fall of 1975, Lorne Michaels and NBC took advantage of this popularity to launch a new show, *NBC's Saturday Night,* the precursor to the show we would all come to know as *Saturday Night Live*. The first episode aired on October 11, and at its 11 p.m. time slot, there was no way I was going to be allowed to stay up to watch it. But I had to try.

On this particular Saturday night, I had successfully convinced Mom that I needed to watch the beginning of *The Carol Burnett Show* that started an hour earlier, thinking if I could make it through that show, I might get to sneak in a few minutes of *NBC's Saturday Night*. I must have fallen asleep at some point during *Carol Burnett* though. Groggy, I came to just in time to hear the theme song for *NBC's Saturday Night* playing in the background. I tried to stay completely still to see if I could watch without anyone knowing, but I was fading in and out.

During a commercial, Mom must have decided she was ready for all the kids to go to bed, because I heard her voice instruct my brother Don to carry me upstairs.

"Don, Darlene fell asleep. Carry her up to her bed, please. Your Dad and I are going to finish watching the show."

I was snuggled on the couch under my favorite afghan, a special gift created just for me by my grandmother. Grandma made an afghan for each one of us kids, but I was convinced mine was the best looking of them all with a pattern of dark blue, medium blue, and light blue crocheted squares all woven together. Wrapping up in it always made me feel particularly special as blue was my favorite color.

Don was fourteen at the time, and I don't remember if he gave a typical teenage grumble or complied without complaint to Mom's request, but I felt his arms slide under me, picking up my afghan-wrapped body. I time traveled as he carried me upstairs and laid me gently in my canopy bed. I imagined myself as Sleeping Beauty in my cream nightgown with the tiny pink bows at the wrists and neck, tucked up under the pastel butterflies of my canopy. I was about to fade off to dreamland for good when I felt a hand on my shoulder.

At first, the hand was exploratory, almost gentle, and in my daze, I thought maybe I was already in a dream. Until the fingers brushed my nipple. My eyes snapped open and I felt heat next to my body, breath on my face, and panic rising in my gut.

Don's face was close to my ear, whispering, "This is okay. Be quiet about it. This is normal. I'm going to do something to you, and you're really going to like it."

Terror filled my belly as his hand started moving away from my chest. I tried to sit up, a scream on my lips before he clapped his other hand over my mouth and, more firmly now, almost menacingly, said, "It's fine, Darlene. It's fine. Just be quiet. This is what brothers and sisters do. It's going to feel good. You're going to like this. We'll have a lot of fun."

Those same words . . . "This is what brothers and sisters do." David's words, but now coming out of a different brother's mouth while he held in my scream and molested my body.

As his hand moved down my rib cage, I thought I was going to throw up. The bile rose in my throat under the weight of his sweaty palm. I started squirming, desperate to get away from his hands. Before I knew what was happening, he moved aside my panties, and slipped a finger inside my vagina.

One finger. Two.

My body went rigid, stiff as a board, but not like our childhood game. I couldn't scream. I couldn't move. I was a statue.

I learned from David that I could never escape, that he would never let me go, so I laid there, still and silent. Suffering.

Until he finished.

Slipping his fingers out of me, he sat up and, saying nothing, headed for my bedroom door. I still hadn't moved an inch, body frozen in shock, cymbals going off in my brain. And then he turned and came back. My mind started yelling "No, no, no, no, no!" but my mouth couldn't get the words out. I felt paralyzed. Leaning down by my left ear, his breath hot against my skin, Don warned, "If you ever tell anybody, no one will believe you. You'll be the one to blame. Mom and Dad will get rid of you because you're dirty. You're going to be destroyed."

Without another word, he turned and walked out, closing the door behind him.

Children are likely to have been subjected to silencing strategies which prevent them from being able to disclose abuse. For example, a child abusing another child may silence them by threatening social isolation or saying they will be in trouble if adults find out.[3]

*   *   *

The tears came as soon as the door shut. For a while, the shock overwhelmed my nervous system, and I was unable to move, talk, or even think. Eventually, I registered that the threat was truly gone, and my body began to loosen. I grabbed for my Holly Hobbie doll, a life-size friend almost as long as me and curled my body around her. I smelled her familiar yarn hair and looked for an answer in her friendly blue eyes, my brain scrambling as I thought, *What am I going to do? What am I going to do?*

For the most part, I had a really good life. I lived in a beautiful home, and I was surrounded by friends, both at school and in the neighborhood. My brother Dale was someone I could count on, and despite Dad's absence at work and Mom's absence for her own reasons, I knew they loved me and cared about me. I didn't want to lose all of the good in my life.

I believed David and Don. I knew if I told Mom and Dad, it would destroy our family. I felt certain my parents would believe me, but for their own reasons, they would cover it up. I would become the "bad girl" who was to blame for causing all of this trouble. They might

---

3   *Child Safety Practice Manual – When a Child Is Sexually Abused by Another Child or Sibling* (Department of Child Safety, Youth and Women, 2024), https://cspm.csyw.qld.gov.au/practice-kits/child-sexual-abuse/working-with-children-who-display-sexually-reactiv/seeing-and-understanding/when-a-child-is-sexually-abused-by-another-child-o.

even ship me away. I didn't want to be an orphan. I wanted to do whatever I could to keep the good part of my family together.

In the quiet of my room, I curled my small body into a tight ball. Tears soaking the blue rectangle afghan, my fingers clenched and unclenched the edge, as if I might find an answer in the opening and closing of my fist. I let out shaky, ragged breaths, my tiny shoulders rising and falling. My grip tightened on Holly. All I wanted was to be comforted, for things to feel safe again. But I knew that wasn't going to happen. I had to make a decision. I had to figure out what I was going to do.

Eyes puffy and red, heart aching, body burning, I made a promise. To my brothers. To myself. To my family.

You can take my childhood. You can steal my innocence.
But you will never ever take my family away from me!

That promise became a secret, one I began to bury inside its own box that night in my bed. I couldn't know in that moment the magnitude of the decision I was making, how *not* telling would impact my life for the next fifty years. All I knew in that moment was that I was going to survive this. I would not allow them to ruin my life.

Shaken, but not broken, I finally fell asleep.

*   *   *

I woke up the next morning and it was as if someone had hit a massive reset button for everyone but me. My family went about their Sunday morning as if life hadn't been permanently altered just hours before. I grabbed a bowl of cereal for breakfast and then wandered into the family room to watch *Johnny Quest* before we had to leave for church. I scooted onto the backseat with Dale and Don for the long drive to church, wondering how I was going to manage to talk to my brother without crying.

But I didn't have a choice. I had to.

I knew my life would never be the same, feel the same, but if I was going to lock down this secret, I had to *act* the same. And as days went by, and then weeks, I got more used to holding the secret, more certain that *not* telling was the only way to protect myself and my family.

But *not* telling is a big job for a little girl. I needed some help to hold that secret, to ensure it didn't swallow me up. At first, I talked to Holly Hobbie. She was there that night, after all, and had seen everything. Holly had brown hair and blue eyes just like me, and she dressed, at least in my mind, like Laura Ingalls from *Little House on the Prairie*. I wanted to be Laura Ingalls so badly, to live that simple life with two sisters, no brothers, tucked into a dugout in Walnut Grove. But that was not my life. I lived here, in a saltbox house in Port Huron, Michigan, with two brothers who had abused me.

I needed to get away from it all, to find some means of being alone that wouldn't put me at risk.

So I started climbing trees. Not just any trees, really, but my tree.

In the mornings, arms wrapped around Holly, the butterflies from my canopy winking me awake, I would stare out the window at my tree. My tree was massive, a giant oak taller than our two-story house. Most of what I could see from that vantage point was its strong, stately trunk, but in the spring and summer, bits of green from the lower branches flashed in the morning sunlight. Its limbs extended well above the height of my window, creating its own canopy of branches to shade the front of our property.

At some point, Dad had nailed two wooden planks horizontally to the bottom part of the tree trunk. I can't remember if I asked him to do it or if he just noticed I was having trouble climbing the tree, but I took advantage all the same. If I lifted my leg as high as it would go, I could just manage to get my foot onto the bottom plank and hoist myself up. At first, I would only climb up to the first layer of branches and hang out, looking at the leaves and the bark like Mom had taught me on our adventures in the woods. It was quiet in the tree, and I felt hidden from the world tucked up in its leaves.

I could hide so well, in fact, that my parents didn't even know I was up there. Oftentimes, my mom would ring the big dinner bell on the outside of our breezeway door or Dad would stick his thumb and forefinger in his mouth to let out a "Come on home!" whistle, not knowing I was literally feet away from them up in my tree. I never called out to them or let them know in any way that I was close by. I loved knowing nobody could find me up in my tree, not my parents, and not Don. I was safe up there.

I eventually got stronger and braver and started climbing higher in the tree. I was determined to reach the very top. Because of how tiny I was, I knew I was the only one that could climb that high safely. If I could get to the top, no one else could follow me. It took months, but eventually, I did it! I was so proud of myself, and boy, was there a view from up there! I would sit in the branches for hours looking out at our neighborhood, seeing neighbors walk by with their dogs, kids playing in our cul-de-sac, listening to the birds sing, and feeling the wind blowing in my face. Perching in the branches felt like I was one step closer to heaven. I would cry. I would laugh. I would pretend I was someone else, and I would dream. The dreaming is what helped me hold on to my sanity. In my tree, I dreamt that I was going to be okay if I could just keep going, if I could bury the pain. If I could hold on to my secret, I could create a different me.

My favorite dream was imagining myself flying with the birds right out of the top of the branches. Maybe things would be better if I could just fly, just get away. Maybe I could hold on to what was down there, the good things with my family, but fly away before the bad things could get me again. Maybe . . .

Maybe it wasn't enough to heal my heart, but it soothed my mind and allowed me to keep going.

The tree became a central figure in my life. It was my sanctuary, my special friend, a place where I could hide from the world but also see it without anyone knowing. In my tree, I was the observer, the looker, the seeker. No one could hunt me up there, because I was the one with the view.

1976, PORT HURON, MICHIGAN. OUR FIRST
CONGREGATIONAL CHURCH FAMILY PHOTO.

4

PORT HURON, MICHIGAN, 1976

Sometimes the best you can do is just remain silent because no words can explain the battle that's going on in your heart and mind.

—UNKNOWN

I vividly remember going to the First Congregational Church when we lived in Connecticut. Even as a five-year-old, the hymns, the pews, the holidays, they all made an impression on me. That's what's so odd about the two years we lived in Clarence; that I recall, we never went to church there. I don't know if my parents just couldn't find one they liked or with five younger kids at home my mom decided it wasn't worth the effort. But once we moved to Port Huron, my family and God made up.

We started attending church regularly almost as soon as we moved. The First Congregational Church of Port Huron was in the city proper, a seven-mile drive from the blue saltbox house on Lakeshore Terrace. My mom had fallen in love with the house and the neighborhood, but both were on the northern outskirts of town, so *everything* we did besides school required a drive. While it probably only took fifteen minutes, as a child, it felt like an eternity. We went to church as a family every Sunday. I don't recall my parents requiring us to go, more so it was just expected that we did. And while the sermons were boring and the old ladies nosey, there were free cookies at coffee hour after the service, and I got to see all of my "town friends," so I generally didn't mind.

The Church became a bedrock of my parents' social standing. My father served on the board and as a liturgist, and my mother became the board treasurer. So many of my memories involve the church from lighting the candles during Advent, to the palm branch processional on Palm Sunday to working the annual craft fair, one of the church's biggest fundraisers. Appearances, and by extension, *my* appearance, especially at church, mattered to my mom. It killed her when I got that Dorothy Hamill "boy" haircut and when I wore pants or jeans to church so I didn't get my nice dresses dirty cleaning up after coffee hour. She felt the need to explain to all of her church friends that it was "Just a phase." On the surface, my brothers, sister, and I were the epitome of a "good Christian family," and my mother worked hard to perpetuate that impression outside the church walls as well.

Given how deeply our family was embedded in church, you might imagine that it would feel like a safe place for me, one where I could tell someone what was going on with my brothers. And I almost did. I intended to talk to our youth minister. At the time, she was probably only in her thirties, but to a ten-year-old, that feels ancient. Standing in front of her, I could feel the words on my tongue, desperate for them to leap into her ears, hope springing that this person could actually help me. That in knowing, she might be able to perform some Jesus-like act of salvation appropriate for a place of worship. Her gentle eyes smiled down on me as I anxiously shifted my weight from one foot to the other. I almost got the words out . . . almost. But Mom's face flashed in my brain. I knew if I told my secret to the woman in front of me, she would have no choice but to tell my mom. I anticipated my mother's reaction, the horror and embarrassment, especially to have this revealed at church. The resulting unease overwhelmed the need to free the secret.

I clamped my mouth shut.

If I couldn't find solace in the members of the church, one might think I could at least find it with God. I did believe in God. Still do, with a lot of caveats. But we were not the kind of family who said nightly prayers on bended knee, hands and heads bowed toward our hearts. In fact, we weren't really the kind of family who brought church home with us at all. But I had been taught that God hears all prayers, and so I did pray, asking God to take me away, to make it stop, to protect my family. I believed that was possible, that if anyone could change my situation, God could. But those prayers seemed to fall on deaf ears. My faith wasn't helping me much in those days, so I decided I had to help myself.

*　　*　　*

I had my first kiss in fourth grade.

His name is so vanilla, it could be an amalgamation of almost any of the white, middle-class names common to boys of that time.

Tommy, Bobby, David, Mike, Jeff. They're all the same, so let's just call him John.

I often went to John's house after school and on the weekends. He had this old-school ping pong table in his garage, and we would bat that little white ball back and forth for hours. His mom was addicted to The Beach Boys and "Barbara Ann" regularly blared from one of her little 45s.

John's neighbor had a treehouse in his backyard. We didn't go up there often, but this one day we had been playing ping pong for hours and were looking for something else to do, so we climbed the ladder to the platform. It wasn't particularly exciting up there, so we just kind of hung out and talked. I don't know who brought it up first, but we started talking about this thing the kids at school were doing. Kissing. Specifically, *French* kissing. I didn't want to let on that I had no idea what it meant. French just sounded fancy and foreign, like my last name DeLoy. John was neither fancy nor foreign, but I was comfortable with him and could tell he was just as baffled as I.

I think I'm the one that said, "Let's just stick our tongues out and see what that does."

I stuck my tongue out, and John skeptically followed suit. We awkwardly shuffled toward each other until the tips of our tongues were touching. Suspended there for a second or two waiting for something magical, we finally made eye contact. We both shrugged, tongues retracting back into our mouths. We weren't repulsed, necessarily, but clearly befuddled by what all the fuss was about. We kind of hugged after that, some show of solidarity or affection, maybe, but it was awkward and we were both desperate to get back to our normal.

"Do you want to go back down and play ping pong?" John asked.

I never once equated that first "French kiss" with John to what I felt in my bedroom that night, Don's hands running all over and inside my body. John's kiss was consensual, I, a willing and knowing participant, had full agency to walk or run away if I wanted to. Don's touch was predatory, his hand over my mouth proof that he understood the sinister nature of his actions. My entire being recognized the difference between experimentation and assault.

I never told my mom about John or my first boyfriend on the church bus or really any interaction I had with a boy. Mom was adamant that I was not to have a boyfriend until I was sixteen. I don't know if she really believed that making that rule would prevent me from messing around with boys or if she could just convince herself that was the truth if she didn't know any different. Regardless, I never told and she never asked, and so the secrets stayed secret.

* * *

While I was playing ping pong with John, Don was trying to establish his own identity in high school.

Sports is where he was most comfortable, having basically grown up on a field or in a gym. He was a solidly average athlete, making the high school football team as a backup defensive back, and playing baseball for the local rec squad. He spent most of his time with two guys from school. The three of them formed a small posse, absorbed into a larger group of kids they hung out with that frequently traveled en masse wherever they went.

Average may actually be the way to describe Don all around. Where I was desperate to be popular, an overachiever, trying to get on everyone's radar as the good girl, it's almost like Don was just trying to fit in. He wasn't hip. He wasn't popular. He wasn't a leader. He wasn't funny. He got average grades and was a decent athlete, but not a standout. He hung out with a popular group of kids, but his identity was wrapped up in being one of them. There was very little about him as an individual that stood out.

I never remember Don bringing a girl to the house. In fact, I never remember Don spending any time with a girl or even seeing him with a girl. My parents teased him relentlessly when he took a basketball to his eighth grade dance instead of a girl, but I could see the appeal. The basketball was under his control, something he knew how to handle. Girls his age were not.

Like many boys in high school, Don was plagued with pervasive acne, inflamed red craters marking his face and neck. It's possible the acne made him insecure, preferring to hide inside the group rather than put himself out there with the ladies. Looking back on this period of his life, I wonder what it must have been like for him, how it could have affected him. His scars were external, flamingly obvious for everyone to see. Mine were hiding on the inside, secret to everyone but him. But scars hurt, no matter where you wear them.

Despite living in the same house, I rarely saw Don. Occasionally on warm weekends, my dad would take us over to Keewahdin Elementary to field balls on the baseball diamond. While Dale and Don were faster and better than me, my summers on the girls hardball team meant I had enough basic skills to participate. While baseball is technically a team sport, during "practice with Dad," we basically stood by ourselves waiting for him to hit the ball our way. Grounders, fly balls, line drives, etc., he would rotate his aim toward each one of us in turn. So, while it could be said that Don and I were playing together, I mostly stayed centerfield, sometimes stepping up to second base, where Don was always at first base. Like most left-handers, he threw a little wonky, but he could catch almost anything coming his way. He was proud of that, and it showed.

I've tried to remember who Don was at fifteen, not what he did, but who he was. I don't know if ten-year-old girls are that aware of their older brothers, their personalities, tendencies, idiosyncrasies, fears. We certainly didn't talk to each other about those things. All I remember is that he is the one who hurt me, but there had to be more to him than that. As an adult, I feel so disconnected from teenage Don. We were siblings, but we may as well have been strangers.

*　　*　　*

I love the beach. The feeling of the sun baking my skin is one of my child-of-the-seventies holdovers. No sunscreen, just UV rays and baby oil. So, the summer after fourth grade, I went to the beach as often as I could. Most days, I went with Freckles, since the beach was essentially her backyard. This one day, though, Freckles wasn't home. Maybe they were on vacation or maybe her mom signed her up for a week of summer camp, who knows, but she wasn't available. I probably could have gotten away with going to her house and hanging out on the beach there even though she wasn't home, but that's weird, right? Right. So, I didn't.

Desmond Beach was a bit of a hike, about a half mile away from our house, so I didn't go there often, but it was a stunning Michigan summer day, and I just wanted to be outside. I packed a hot pink towel into my cream sling bag and put a thin cover up on over my favorite yellow bikini. At ten, I felt so adult in this swimsuit. The color of the sun itself, the top of the bikini was a tube with a tiny scrunch in the middle. Carrying the look down to the bottoms, there was more scrunching, with bright yellow strings dangling down the sides of my thighs that I would tie into small bows right at my hip.

Ready to go, I left a note for my mom. By the time I was ten, all of the other kids were either out of the house or teenagers, so Mom had given up hope of keeping track of all of us. That meant I pretty much could go where I wanted. The only rule was I had to leave a note detailing where I would be and when I was planning to be back. That accomplished, I headed out for the beach.

Alone on the beach, I laid my towel down and applied a mix of baby oil and iodine, all the rage with the teenage girls of the day to get the deepest, darkest tan. Skin cancer wasn't really a thing yet. Having been out on the beach for awhile, I was starting to sweat, beads of salty liquid sliding down my chest and under the edge of my tube top. Despite all of us being good swimmers, we were never allowed to swim alone in the lake, only wade in up to our knees, so my options for cooling off were limited. But, I was about to get up to go down and splash water on myself when I felt a shadow pass over my face. I opened one eye, covering the other with my hand to find Don staring down at me.

"What are you doing here?" I asked, as I certainly hadn't invited him and honestly had no idea how he knew where I was.

"Your note," he said casually.

I wasn't immediately alarmed. At that point, it had been almost a year since the incident in my bedroom and Don hadn't made a single attempt to touch me since. Granted, I worked hard to never be in this exact situation, alone with him, but we were in a public place out on the beach, so surely I was safe.

Don started drawing pictures in the sand with a stick close to where I had laid out my towel. For a while, we took turns, handing the stick back and forth to each other while we added details to his picture. The sun started to dip in the sky, the angle of light across our pictures getting longer.

Eventually, Don said, "Come on. It's getting late. Mom's expecting us to be home for dinner."

I shook the sand off my towel and packed it and my baby oil back in my little cream bag. Sticky with sweat and sand, I was reluctant to put my cover up back on, but I knew Mom would be livid to find out I had walked all the way home in just my bikini, so I pulled it over my head and tried to keep it from plastering to my body. Following behind Don, we started trudging up the sand toward the grassy path that led back to our house. My legs were five years shorter than his, so I was a fair distance back when he said, "Hey look! I found something. Come over here!" Every now and again we would find geodes broken open along the line of rocks and brush separating the sand from the grass. The geodes were a deep purple inside, each unique with their array of glimmering crystals tucked up inside the rock's shell. "Rock crystals" we used to call them. I loved rock crystals. Assuming that's what Don had found, I rushed up to where he was standing, pointing at the ground with his stick. I must have moved in front of him to get a better look because the next second I was on the ground. He pushed me to my knees and flipped me over onto my back. A wrestling move of sorts, it was fast and effective.

He put his knees on my shoulders, pinning me down under his weight as one of his hands pulled the bottoms of my favorite yellow bikini down over my hips.

Desmond Beach is not a tourist beach. There are a few houses separated by big yards and one secluded tree-covered gully that leads back to the main road. There was no one in sight.

Knowing this, I writhed and screamed anyway, trying to get Don off of me. I must have been making too much noise because he put his hand, his left hand, over my mouth again. Holding me down with the weight of his body, he slipped his penis out of the front flap of his bathing suit.

There, right next to Desmond Beach, I lost my virginity.

It sounds like a romantic story when I say it that way. But it wasn't. It was rape.

*   *   *

I remember it being over not much after it started, like my only job was the release. I lay flat on my back as he climbed off of me, tears running down my temples into the sandy grass, his threats ringing in my ears.

"Get up," he said. "We have to go."

I slowly pulled up the bottoms of my favorite yellow bikini and started to stand up. Don grabbed my arm, trying to propel me to go faster, as I picked up my cream beach bag from where it lay next to my body.

"We have to come home together. Mom's expecting us to come home together," he said, emphatic and slightly manic, although with complete lack of acknowledgement of what he had just done.

He started walking away from me. Not knowing if I could walk, the pain in my body searing and the kaleidoscope in my head exploding, I slowly put one flip-flopped foot in front of the other. Don kept looking back, making sure I was behind him as he picked up speed when his feet found the black top. I could hear the cars rushing by on Lakeshore Road. So close to safety. So close . . . but not close enough.

I don't know how I made it home.

Still sandy from laying out and dirty in ways and places I had never experienced before, I went to shower. Don had already claimed the shower in the kids bathroom, so I went to my parents' room. When the water warmed enough for me to climb in, I put my back against the tile wall and let my knees finally give out. Sinking to the floor, I watched the fading light of the day turn the beige tile a gentle blue.

For a while, I just sat there, water beating down on my shoulders, staring blankly at the green Prell shampoo bottle sitting on the shower bench. Anger, fear, and bitterness bumped up against total exhaustion inside my addled brain. Almost trance-like, I rubbed the bar of soap methodically across the wash cloth, lather building as my hands moved faster. I began to scrub.

I attacked my body like it was at fault, its dirtiness an enemy I had to overcome. I scrubbed and scrubbed until my skin burned, the sting from the water a welcome reminder that I was making progress. Once I had cleaned the actual dirt and sand from my back and butt, I turned to cleaning the inside of me. But I couldn't get clean. Tears mixing with the shower's cascade, I scrubbed, but I just knew. I would never be clean again. I would always be tainted. And now, just like they said, I really was dirty.

It is common for families to use strategies of minimization when SSA is disclosed, including believing that it never happened or that it was normal play or curiosity. In some families, this minimization may present as cutting the abused child off from love or affection or blaming them for what happened.[4]

---

4   Amy Adams, "Family Characteristics, Responses, and Dynamics Associated with Sibling Sexual Abuse: A Scoping Review," *Child Abuse and Neglect* 162, part 3 (2025), https://doi.org/10.1016/j.chiabu.2024.106795.

THE TREE-COVERED GULLY
LEADING TO DESMOND BEACH.

1978. ME IN MY SEVENTH GRADE SOCCER UNIFORM.

5

PORT HURON, MICHIGAN, 1976–1978

Give me back my girlhood. It was mine first.
—TAYLOR SWIFT

I had done a good job of hiding my girlness in elementary school. My Dorothy Hamill bob and tomboy tendencies often made people guess that I was another one of the DeLoy boys. There was relative safety in not being noticed, but as I neared the beginning of fifth grade, my body started to betray me.

I grew boobs. Big boobs.

The kind of boobs that couldn't be hidden by normal fifth grade attire. One day at recess, I was wearing what, for me, was a rather frilly top with cap sleeves and pink, light blue, and yellow stripes around the neck and edge of the sleeves. It had a seam that ran right underneath my chest, and, likely the biggest culprit, a V-neck. A competitive game of kickball was underway, and it was my turn to kick. Not to brag, but those early years in sports had developed a natural athleticism in me, and kickball was my jam. The ball came full speed toward me, and I landed a perfect kick to the outfield. I took off, running as fast as I could around the bases. As I rounded third base, I felt the eyes of the other kids on me. Jogging into home base, I heard the recess monitor blow the whistle that signaled the return back to class. Breathing heavily, I started walking toward the building with the other kids. That's when I heard it . . . the murmur. Pockets of kids covering their mouths with their hands and not so subtly staring right at me while they whispered something in their neighbor's ear. I finally caught what one of them was saying.

"Oh my gosh! Look at her boobs! They're bouncing all over the place in that shirt!"

The color started right where they were looking and crept up my neck to my cheeks. I was mortified. I spent the rest of the day trying to shrink into my desk, doing everything in my power to hold back the tears. The second school was out, I rushed home and told Mom that I needed a bra. She was skeptical but must have somewhat agreed as she went to the store and came back with the soft, pliable training bras that the other little girls were starting to wear. One look at me in just a training bra, my B cups spilling over the top and nipples pressing against the fabric, and she returned to the store for a real bra.

In contrast, all of my friends were trying to make their breasts grow bigger, or at all. *Are you there God? It's Me, Margaret,* Judy Blume's classic novel on the transition from girlhood to adolescence was published in 1970, and the iconic scene from Nancy's bedroom played out in bedrooms across America in the summer of 1976.

"We must! We must! We must increase our bust!" chanted my friends as they voraciously thrust their elbows backward like chicken wings, sticking their less-than A cups out in hopes this ridiculous exercise would accelerate puberty.

I was desperately hoping for the opposite. Maybe if I thrust my elbows in, squeezing my chest as close together as possible, I could reverse what was happening to my body.

*　*　*

Because of my aggressive development, I was even more desperate to fit in. My two best girlfriends at the time, Cozie and Winnie, were the most popular girls at school. For a while, we were like the three amigos, always together. I even trusted them enough to invite them to play in my tree, the three of us pretending to be Charlie's Angels. Winnie had short black hair at the time so insisted she had to play Kate Jackson. I always wanted to be Jaclyn Smith, and Cozie didn't seem to care much so she took on the role of Farrah Fawcett. It's interesting to me that I was comfortable playing the role of any sex symbol given how uncomfortable I was with male attention. I absolutely did not want to be Farrah for this very reason, but the '70s was a pivotal decade for feminism, and the Angels were generally portrayed as intelligent, competent, and able to handle themselves without a man, which were all things I wanted to be.

But I didn't have Jaclyn Smith's self-confidence in real life, and it showed when I started trying to be exactly like Cozie and Winnie. Winnie's father was a well-respected physician in town and her family was quite wealthy. As a result, she was constantly getting new clothes and shoes and accessories to wear to school. Our classmates looked to her to set the tone for what trendy meant in fifth grade. I decided I needed to be just like Winnie in order to stay in her good graces. So, when she wore a new outfit to school, I would beg my mother to go buy the same one or at least a close knock off. Winnie had extremely small feet, a size 5 or so, but my already developing body shot my feet out to a full 7.5 adult size. I would cram my feet into the smallest shoes I could manage so they looked just a little more like Winnie's, wincing as I walked, but feeling more confident in my coolness.

The final straw was the day Winnie wore a new pair of shoes to school. Brown penny loafers. That very afternoon I pleaded with my mom to go to the store and get the exact same pair. I just had to have those shoes. I have no idea why my mother agreed to this, but she clearly must have seen my desperation and thought there was a good reason. Carrying the new shoes in their rectangular box, I proudly walked over to Winnie's to show her that we could now match.

Cozie was at Winnie's house when I got there. I popped open the lid of the new shoe box to show them, and a look of absolute disgust came over Winnie's face. I don't remember what they said, but I do remember I didn't get farther than the front door. The mean words that came out of both of them sent me running back home, tears flying.

Of course, Mom was insistent I wear the new shoes she just bought me to school the next day. To make matters worse, she wanted me to wear pantyhose instead of tights, perhaps out of some misplaced pride that I finally looked like a young woman instead of a tomboy. A small leather purse completed the look. I knew this was a bad idea, but I couldn't explain to her why I didn't want to wear the shoes or the hose or the purse. I went to school hoping that maybe the humiliation had ended with their harsh words the day before.

I was wrong.

I left my purse on my desk in the classroom during recess. When I came back, there was something in it. A note. The words scrawled in little-girl handwriting were far worse than the ones hurled at me the day before, the insults an echo of David and Don's words . . . "You think you're so cool, but you're not. You're just trash. Nothing but a piece of dirt."

I hid my tears that day, but I couldn't hide the hurt. Maybe they were right. Maybe I was worthless.

That was the first time I thought about ending my life.

*　　*　　*

I never thought I would actually like boys in any sort of romantic way. My fourth grade "boyfriend," John, was my best friend, and while the other kids teased us about being a couple, that one botched attempt at French kissing was our only semi-intimate moment. But as fifth grade fell away to middle school, I started to see boys differently.

When I began experimenting with boys, I was always terrified my mom would find out. Her rule was clear—no boyfriends until I was sixteen—but her negative reaction when I tried to talk to her about John sparked some of my own defiance. If she didn't want to hear about my feelings for boys, I vowed to never tell her *anything* about anyone I was interested in.

Duke Alexander IV was the most gorgeous boy I had ever seen. He was popular and smart, athletic and funny. He also happened to be black, which had no bearing on my interest in him, but was a big deal in the 1970s in small-town Michigan. In sixth grade, we started dating, which basically meant we would hang out at our lockers together before school started and sit together at school assemblies. He never came to my house, and I never went to his, but to us, we were boyfriend and girlfriend. I liked Duke, and I felt safe with him.

My mom was a substitute teacher at our middle school at the time. My guess is that someone ratted me out because when we got home one afternoon, Mom told me she'd heard something about me at school that day and asked if it was true. I couldn't tell if she was more disappointed that I had disobeyed her boyfriend rule or more incredulous that the boyfriend was black, but she was less than pleased. I skirted around my response, trying to change the subject so I didn't have to lie to her. The very next day, I picked a fight with Duke, and we broke up. It may have been after the fact, but sabotaging my relationship ensured that what I told my mother was, in fact, true. This one act started a long line of tanking perfectly good relationships for a variety of perfectly awful reasons.

I didn't want to talk to Mom about boys because I knew I wasn't supposed to be in a relationship with them, at least according to her. But even more so, I didn't want *her* to talk to *me* about boys because I was terrified I might slip up and tell her about Don. The words sat just behind my lips, always threatening to pop out. I knew that conversations about boys, any boys, but especially that boy, were off limits with Mom.

*　　*　　*

Society has this ignorant assumption that if you have big boobs, you must be a slut. That assumption and the fact that my brothers taught me to accept whatever was done to me without resistance meant I was woefully unprepared to navigate my early experiences with adolescent boys.

In seventh grade, the most popular party game was Five Minutes in the Closet. Looking back, twelve seems inordinately young to have any idea what to do with those five minutes, but I guess some people had done their homework. One weekend, I was invited to a sleepover. Four or five of us seventh grade girls piled up in the host's family room watching the first *Halloween* movie. As I recall, my girlfriend's parents were out for the night, assuming we were well entertained. Everything was going fine until the boys showed up. Turns out, one of the girls that was spending the night had a boyfriend in eighth grade. Upon learning her parents weren't home, he and his buddies decided to stop by. One of them suggested we play Five Minutes in the Closet. Nervous, but not wanting to stand out, I dutifully sat down to participate. I escaped the first few rounds, but statistics were not in my favor. A few spins in, the fated bottle landed on me. Witt, the spinner, looked up and half smiled. He got to his feet, and I hesitantly followed him toward the closet as the other kids snickered. I had no idea what to do.

But Witt did.

I laid there while he moved his hands all over my body and stuck his fingers up my skirt. I guess I was a willing participant, although I had been groomed to do whatever I was told to. Witt wasn't aggressive or mean. There were no threats following his fingering. But it still felt like a violation. I didn't know you could resist. Didn't know it was an option to say "No more. STOP." I didn't realize you could have that kind of agency with a boy.

Monday morning, the fact that Witt went to third base with Darlene in the closet at the party on Saturday was all over school. I don't know if Witt was the one that told, proud of his conquest, or if the rumor got started and was never denied, but, once again, I was mortified.

Conditioning runs deep. I knew how to pretend that I was fine, how to continue the ruse, so I gathered my pride and accepted Witt's invitation the following weekend to join him and his eighth grade friends for a bonfire. When I arrived, everyone was outside, but I wasn't friends with any of these upperclassmen, so I stuck close to Witt. It started sprinkling, and I began to hope that the whole thing would be called off, but instead, everyone huddled closer to the bonfire to keep warm. Witt ran inside to grab a raincoat. He brought his sister's raincoat out for me to try, but it was too small. More than a sprinkle by this point, I was getting wetter and wetter by the minute. We went inside to find me something to wear, but Witt didn't want to get his mom's raincoat wet. Thinking fast, he told me that his friends often used trash bags as raincoats with a hole cut in the top for the head to poke through. Not seeing any other choice, I accepted the offer, and donned my plastic trash bag rain coat. Witt and I walked back outside together to the bonfire.

As soon as we approached, I heard the coughs . . . one after the other, the coughs turned to barely concealed giggles. Pretty soon, I heard the word clearly, the coughs no longer concealing the dig. Cough—"Trash"—Cough—Giggle—Giggle. I was sick to my stomach.

All I could think is here we go again. I am living with the actions of what my brothers have done to me, but now in public. These kids have figured out who I really am. Trash.

I whipped around and walked back into Witt's house, ripping off my trashbag as I moved. I called my parents to come get me and then defiantly stood on Witt's front porch waiting for them to arrive. Witt begged me to come back inside where it was warm and dry, but I refused. Standing there, shivering, all I wanted was to get out of there.

I wanted to go home and then keep going, to somewhere permanent, somewhere not here. I don't know that I actually wanted to kill myself as much as I just wanted the pain to stop. I wanted to silence the voices in my head, always echoing David and Don's words, and now those of the other kids at school. I always came back to my family though—Mom, Dad, Diane, and Dale. I knew my suicide would devastate them, and the whole point of keeping this secret was to keep them all together. So I didn't kill myself. I pushed it down, shoving all of the hurt and pain and anger into the box on top of the secret I was keeping. I slammed the lid shut and locked it tight.

But, the box started to leak.

* * *

Despite being in middle school, I became increasingly afraid to walk anywhere alone, day or night. It started with running home to avoid the darkening sky, but it got worse. I always felt like someone was stalking me, watching me.

During the summers when we roamed free in the neighborhood, there were nightly games of flashlight tag. The It person would stand in the middle of the road. After giving us a countdown warning, he or she would shine the flashlight all around, trying to get the beam of light to cross one of our bodies to tag us out. There were streetlights that offered a little illumination, but otherwise, it was pitch black on our street. I didn't want to be left out of the game, and I certainly didn't want to be alone at home, but I couldn't play by myself. The second all of the kids would scatter in the dark, the terror would creep up my spine, constricting my lungs, causing a cold sweat to break out over my entire body. I attached myself to my brother Dale, ensuring when he ran, I went with him. We always hid together, which meant I was almost always responsible for getting us both out, but it was the only way I could play without panicking.

This wasn't the only place where I seemed to be regressing, where my increasing age and my behavior were going in opposite directions. I started having nightmares. The same nightmare, night after night. It started with me asleep in my bed, awakened by something I couldn't identify—a noise, a sense, a light. I would peek out my window and see men dressed entirely in black, masks pulled over their faces, hovering all around our house. They crept toward our house and started looking in the basement windows. Glass shattered as they kicked open one of the windows. I didn't stay to watch their entry as I searched for a place to hide. I ran into our hallway and used all of my strength to pull on the rope cord attached to the attic door in the hallway ceiling. I slid the wooden stairs toward me as quietly as possible and scampered up into the attic. With strength only possible in dreamland, I pulled the stairs up behind me and silently shut the door. I crawled to the farthest corner of the attic, curling myself into a tiny ball. No matter how far back I went, they would always find me. I could see their bodies coming toward me, hunting me, closing in. And then I would wake up.

Sweating, panting, heart racing, there was no way I was going back to sleep in my own bed. I tiptoed down the hall to my parents room, turning the old gold knob silently, and slipping in behind the door. I would make a place for myself between my parents, snuggling in to their safety. Only then would my pulse calm and my eyes close, only then could I sleep without fear that the men would come back.

I'd wake to find my dad on the floor next to the bed, pillow under his head and a throw blanket covering him. My twelve-year-old body was no longer small enough to fit comfortably in their queen-sized bed with them, so rather than wake me up to go back to bed, he would just move to the floor.

Night after night, I snuck into my parents' room. They asked what the problem was, of course. I told them I was having nightmares, but that's all I would say, the details of the nightmare another one of my closely kept secrets. Looking back, I wonder why they didn't press harder, worry more, investigate deeper. Even purely just to stop having to sleep on the floor, I wonder why they never tried to get to the bottom of those nightmares, to help me get over them.

But they didn't, and I've had nightmares ever since.

1982. Lulu and me, sophomores at
Port Huron Northern High School.

6

PORT HURON, MICHIGAN, 1979–1984

She was brave, and strong, and broken all at once.

—ANNA FUNDER

The summer after eighth grade was a time of experimentation. With not a lot to do in our sleepy Midwestern town and a whole lot of freedom, it was inevitable that we'd fill that space with something else. We were headed to high school, which meant we had to up our game in order to hang with the older kids. We knew that acceptance and, at least in high school terms, survival were on the line.

I got high for the first time at church camp that summer. The girls from the other middle school across town were there too, and they came prepared. One of those girls had been my bestie the previous two summers, but this year she brought along her two closest friends from her school, so we became a group of four. I was grateful to not be the odd man out in a classic three girl triangle, but I often felt like I existed just on the periphery. I remember one night, we snuck out of our cabin and walked around, wandering aimlessly until we found our way down to the lake. It was one of those memorable July nights in Michigan: warm, lake still as glass, the moon illuminating our steps and making art of the water.

Right in the middle of the gravel path, one of the girls whispered, "Hey guys, I brought something from home," as she slung her backpack around to her chest and pulled out a metal box with something wrapped in tissue inside. I thought it was a cigarette, but the smell quickly belied its true identity. I had never smoked pot before, but they assured me all the girls at their school were doing it. The first time the joint went around the circle, I guiltily passed, but when it came around again, they egged me on. I was super scared, but following their instructions, I took a tiny puff. Immediately, I started gagging and coughing and carrying on, loud enough to wake the entire camp, but no one came out of their cabins. The girls giggled, nodding their approval, and I breathed a marijuana-tinged sigh of relief at having passed their test.

The irony is not lost on me. In my mom's effort to make all of us appear to be the good, church-going family, she introduced me to a world equally as flawed and messed up as our own. It, too, was a world that was adept at keeping secrets.

* * *

The first few weeks of ninth grade were excitingly angsty as we all adjusted to the new world order. The popular girls talked about nothing but their exploits that summer, and all of their stories somehow involved when they got their period. Elaborate tales of blood on car seats and being scared sharks would sniff them out at the beach and pads and tampons and womanhood. Despite my large boobs, I had not gotten my period yet and was incredibly self-conscious about that fact. I wanted to be a popular girl. Couldn't my body help me out just a little?

The other thing that became "normal" that summer was shaving your legs. While none of us had more than peach fuzz on our legs, apparently there had been a collective decision that summer that peach fuzz was no longer acceptable. We needed smooth, tanned, elegant legs for ninth grade. This, at least, was one thing I had control over.

I knew my mom shaved her legs with an electric razor. I could hear it periodically as I walked past their bedroom, buzzing loudly from inside her bathroom. But there was no way I was going to ask Mom how to use it. I knew she would tell me I was too young anyway.

My parents purchased a Christian bookstore in 1978 or 1979. Mom ran it, and all of us kids worked there after school and on weekends to earn money. The store was open daily until 5 p.m., so when it wasn't my afternoon to work, there were a few hours after school when I usually had the house to myself. That was my window. Despite being alone in the house, I tiptoed into Mom's bathroom and shut the door behind me. I think I might have even locked it to give me time to stow the contraband should I hear someone coming in during my experiment. I rooted around in the cabinet under her sink until I found the white box that housed her pale blue Lady Remington razor. Dressed in my favorite brown corduroy jumper with tights underneath, I shimmied out of the tights and hiked the jumper up around my waist so I could sit on the orange and brown shag carpet next to the outlet.

I plugged the razor into the wall and turned it on . . . bzzzzzzzz.

I carefully slid the razor up and down my legs, using toilet paper to wipe off the trimmed hair. My heart pounded both from the fear of cutting myself and from the anxiety of being discovered. When I was done, I slowly ran my hands up and down my freshly shaved legs. There were a few spots that clearly needed an extra pass, but overall, I was pretty pleased with myself. And I liked how my legs felt without hair. Soft and smooth, like a woman's legs.

I quickly cleaned up, carefully putting all of the pieces to the razor back in their individual compartments inside the white box and shoving it back under the sink. I grabbed my shoes and tights, looking around the bathroom to make sure there was no additional evidence and, satisfied I was in the clear, turned the knob to open the door.

Don was standing in my parents' bedroom.

Startled, I said, "What are you doing in here?"

His look alarmed me. I knew that look. "It's play time again," he said, closing the distance between us.

He threw me on our parents' bed, trapping me with his knees on my shoulders as I screamed and cried, "Why are you doing this?!?" The infamous arm bar clapped me down on the bed as he used his other hand to pull down my underwear. His eighteen-year-old body, now far more like a man's than a boy's, was bigger and heavier than I remember, and as he penetrated me, I felt a physical pain that I had not experienced the times before.

It was quick, aggressive, and almost angry. And then it was over. I wish I could say I fought him, but I didn't. Fighting had never worked. Screaming had never worked. So I lay there, staring at the white popcorn ceiling, just waiting for it to be over. Don's hot breath rasped his normal threats in my ear, and then he was up, off of me, and out of the room.

I got up off the bed, tears running down my face, but numb. I looked at my parents bed, wrinkled and matted from our bodies. I straightened it quickly, putting the pillows back in place, erasing the evidence of what had just happened to me. I went back into their bathroom and sat on the toilet, willing every last drop of him to drain out of me. I just wanted it all to come out. My mom had a douche kit under her sink. I saw it when I was looking for the razor. I grabbed the douche kit and read the directions. Following the pictures on the fold out paper, I tried desperately to get clean. I wanted to throw up. I wanted to scream. I wanted to escape.

But, I didn't. I cleaned up, put the box with the remnants of the douche kit in my closet so Mom wouldn't find it, and went back to pretending life in my house was normal, whatever that meant.

Sibling sexual abuse can involve more invasive, coercive, and lengthy sexual abuse than child sexual abuse by a nonfamily member—all factors that are associated with worse outcomes.[5]

*　　*　　*

Public schools in the state of Michigan were in dire trouble in 1979. The State School Aid Act of 1979 was intended to correct this problem,

---

5   Hannah McDowell et al., "Children Exposed to Sibling Sexual Abuse: Sociodemographic and Trauma Symptom Differences," *Child Abuse and Neglect* 162, part 3 (2025), https://doi.org/10.1016/j.chiabu.2024.107149.

providing the framework to allocate funding to public schools as well as community colleges and universities in the state. However, local municipalities were left to their own devices to determine how to pay for extracurricular activities in their schools.

Unfortunately, the voters in Port Huron were reluctant to pass any bill that increased their taxes. In 1979, when the school millage failed to pass, it had devastating consequences for the Port Huron Area School District. All extracurricular activities were defunded— no sports, no library; no art, choir, or band. Families scrambled, trying to figure out how to keep their kids in sports, particularly those that were college prospects. Many families moved to be able to attend schools in different districts, and some even moved to Canada to finish high school. Additionally, individuals with the last names A–J went to school from 6 a.m. to noon and L–Z went from 1 p.m. to 7 p.m. It was a mess.

It didn't help that the one hang out spot we had, the parking lot at Lakeside Beach & Park, was also quickly made off limits. During my early years in high school, we spent Friday and Saturday nights at the Park, cars parked row after row with high school kids from freshmen to seniors. It was an amazing way to meet other kids in all different grades. At the time, we really weren't doing anything other than hanging out and talking, although some kids were definitely drinking or getting high in their cars. It may seem odd to say, but at least we were all there together. If one of us snuck down to the lake to make out with a boy, there were a bunch of other girls watching out for her. We may not have always been doing the right thing, but what we were doing was pretty tame. It seems inevitable, however, that when adults observe a bunch of teenagers in the same place at the same time, the singular conclusion is that they must be making trouble. So, eventually, the town leaders took the passive aggressive approach of making it illegal to park in the lot after hours, effectively shutting down our hang out spot.

With no place to gather and nothing to do, drugs and alcohol filled the void, accelerated by our proximity to the Canadian border where the legal drinking age was nineteen.

Understanding that boredom is the bedfellow of bad decisions for teenagers, my parents saw the value in keeping me in cheerleading, so they paid the additional fee for me to be a part of the team. Like church camp, however, the unintended consequence of that decision was that I was now part of a club where drugs and alcohol were the norm, and where I was expected to do both to belong. So, it didn't take much coaxing for me to try mescaline the first time it was offered to me. We were at Jules' house, hanging out with other girls from the cheerleading squad and some of the upperclassmen guys who wanted to see the "fresh meat."

Gil, always the supplier, produced a bag of pills from somewhere and pulled Jules and her best friend aside first, asking if they wanted to try it. Then it was my best friend Lulu's turn, and then mine. Gil offered each of us one pill, but we were all pretty hesitant, so together we convinced him to break it into four equal parts. He put a single pill on the counter and, giving us crap for being such weenies, used a butter knife to slice it up for us.

Mescaline is the active ingredient in peyote, a naturally occurring hallucinogenic. Frankly, the idea of hallucinating sounded pretty good to me, especially if it allowed me to escape the constant feelings of insecurity and shame. I hoped my trip might be like some of the crazy experiences Gil told us about—vivid colors, talking animals, flying away. For the first fifteen minutes, nothing happened, so we just kept drinking beer. But suddenly, I did start seeing colors, and I had a hard time speaking, like my mouth was literally zipped shut even though my brain wanted to speak. Unfortunately, the rest of my trip was not so enjoyable. The mescaline only enhanced my sadness and paranoia. I hated myself for what happened to me. The shame pounded through me, almost as if the drug gave it its own sound. Eventually, I got so upset that I went outside and hid in the bushes to cry by myself.

*　　*　　*

While hallucinogens may not have had the desired effect of blurring my memories and dulling my pain, alcohol did. And there was alcohol everywhere.

With nothing to do before or after school, kids were drinking around the clock, and that was to say nothing of the parties. This was long before drunk-driving deaths and litigation put the legal onus on parents if there were minors drinking on their watch, so it was not unusual back then for parents to sanction a party at their own house. Looking back, it was probably an effort to keep their kids safe, knowing that they were going to be drinking whether they were at home or not.

It was at one of these parties that I became the Mellow Yellow girl.

Rosie was the all-American girl in high school—cheerleader, Homecoming court, funny, nice, and down to earth. Not to mention movie-star pretty. Everyone loved her. I just wanted to be near her, hoping some of her belonging might transfer to me.

Rosie lived in a small ranch house off of a busy road, but her family owned acres of the land that the house sat on, making it perfect for parties. Her dad built a bonfire on the back acre, and before long, high schoolers with cases of beer magically appeared. It was an iconic "If you build it, they will come" moment.

Everyone got drunk. There was no such thing as casual drinking in my high school. We drank to get drunk, period. I just wanted to fit in, just wanted to belong, just wanted to be part of the club. So I got drunk too.

Standing around the bonfire, I noticed someone drinking a Mellow Yellow. Turns out, it was actually half Mellow Yellow, half vodka, and they were more than happy to share. Alcohol alters your sense of humor, making the most mundane things hilarious, especially at fifteen. My vodka-spiked brain attached itself to those words . . . "Mellow. Yellow." I couldn't stop repeating them, slowly, emphasizing the meeeee-llllooooowwwww. I went around the party, holding my can up high, asking everyone I saw, "Hey! Do you want to get Mellow with me?" and laughing hysterically at their confused faces.

I ended up on the living room floor making out with a boy while the remnants of the partygoers stepped around us. It wasn't a good look. But it was memorable, and my entire high school career, me and Mellow Yellow made a name for ourselves.

*　*　*

Pete and I met at a bar. Based on what I've told you already, that should be no surprise. Except this bar was in Canada. You didn't need a passport to cross the border back in those days, just a driver's licence and thirty-five cents each way to cross the Blue Water Bridge. Once we turned sixteen, Lulu and I took advantage of the town-documents fixer and bought ourselves fake IDs. Nineteen was the legal drinking age in Canada, and it was far easier to convince a bouncer of that three-year spread than to take our chances in the States. We drove across the border to Sarnia to a well known hang out spot, Campbell Street Station.

I'd like to say it was love at first sight, but it may have been more like lust or just attention from a cute boy at first sight. We caught each other's eye across the room and what started as fleeting glances ended up as dancing all night on the sticky wooden dance floor. I was sixteen and he was eighteen, the same year in school as my brother Dale.

All of the drinking and drugs were starting to take their toll on me. I was embarrassed, ashamed, and losing friends as a result. Pete offered a safe harbor in the storm. For the next two years, I leaned in to him almost exclusively, shutting out the rest of the world in favor of this cocoon the two of us created.

After a year of dating, Pete wanted to have sex. We never openly talked about it, at least not with the actual word *sex*, but it was obvious that he wanted things to progress. I was reticent, both because of my past experiences with intercourse but also because I was terrified he would find out I wasn't a virgin. When he invited me to spend the night at his house the next time his parents were out of town, I said yes. I must have known where it would lead, but it still took a bit of coaxing. Pete told me we could just lay in bed together without having sex, which we did. But then he put his hand between my legs. I wanted to make him happy, so when he raised his eyebrows at me, looking for my consent to go further, I nodded.

Having sex with Pete cracked the box of my secrets. It was so different than my other experiences to date. He asked. He was gentle. He used a condom. He apologized for hurting me. He told me he loved me.

The one similarity was that when it was over, I cried. Bawled, in fact. Pete was so thrown off, concerned that he had hurt me. I couldn't let him think that my reaction was his fault, so consumed by the moment, I let the secret slip out. I told him. I admitted to being dirty, tainted, and I apologized for not being the pure virgin he thought I was. I so wanted him to be my first, and I was so ashamed that he wasn't. I swore him to silence, inviting him and the secret back into the box with me.

But now I knew. I *could* be loved. I *could* be special. I may be tainted, but I didn't have to be a victim.

*   *   *

It may seem like a minor miracle that I even made it through high school, but I actually graduated on time with pretty decent grades. If it wasn't for math and social studies, I might have been a straight A student. And while I knew I wanted to go to college, I had no idea where I wanted to go or what I wanted to do. I felt bad wasting my parents' money on my uncertainty, so I decided to stay at home and go to the local community college until I figured some things out. I basically had the house to myself anyway. Dale was away at college and Don had moved into an apartment about twenty minutes from our house. He was dating a woman four years older than him who had a young baby. Despite all of his friends' reservations, he was intent on marrying her. I'm not sure that I much cared what he did as long as he stayed away from me.

That day, I was in my room, rushing to finish getting ready, already running a few minutes late to meet all of my friends for our nightly trip over the border. Throwing my bag over my shoulder, I double timed it down the stairs, already envisioning grabbing my keys from the key rack on the wall by the breezeway door. I hit the bottom of the stairs and turned left and came to a dead halt.

Don stood in the family room. I hadn't heard him come in. He still had a key, of course, but I couldn't think of a single reason he needed to be here.

I felt the hairs on the back of my neck stand up and panic rising in my chest.

Don could see the look of confusion on my face. He said, "Hey. I'm just here to pick up some of my stuff that's still in my old closet." I nodded, moving slowly to try and get past him.

Almost conversationally, casually, he said, "You know, we should do what we used to do."

My jaw dropped, but this time rage replaced the fear. I yelled, "Are you kidding me?!? You think I enjoyed that? You are a sick fuck! Do not ever talk to me about this again. Do not ever approach me again. And GET OUT OF THIS HOUSE!"

Shaking, I rushed past him, grabbed my keys, and jogged to my car. I peeled out of the driveway, still breathing hard, the adrenaline coursing through my veins.

I couldn't believe it. I was nineteen; Don was twenty-four and about to get married. It had been six years since the last time he raped me and nothing, nothing since then. How could he possibly think I *wanted* to have sex with him? That I was ever anything but his victim?

But there was something else I couldn't believe. I stood up to him. I said no more. Adult Darlene was not a little girl anymore. She could fight back. She could protect herself. She could choose.

That was the last we spoke of it. At least for forty years . . .

Part II

The Princess Has Problems

1989, East Lansing, Michigan. Dani, Bethany, and I heading out to dinner.

7

MICHIGAN STATE UNIVERSITY, 1985–1990

If you want to know who your tribe is, speak your truth and see who sticks around. Those are yours.

—SISTER SHANTI

I lasted a year at SC4—St. Clair County Community College. I definitely hadn't yet figured out what I wanted to do, but I secured a $500 grant and that felt like doing my part, so off to Michigan State University (MSU) I went.

If I was at all apprehensive about leaving home, those fears quickly subsided with the realization that dorm life at MSU was one ongoing party. I lived in Akers Hall those first two years, and I'm not sure there was a single moment I was ever alone. Akers is set up so that on the fourth floor, the girls live on the right side and the boys on the left. It was like a permanent Chinese fire drill with how often we changed beds, girls on the boys side, and vice versa. Most of us weren't actually sleeping around; we just passed out in whoever's bed was closest or whomever seemed most appealing in our current state.

I was always concerned with being able to take care of myself, and that meant making my own money, so when I got to Michigan State, I took a job at the front desk of the dorm. What was a mindless operation for them became a fantastic way for me to meet people! Including boys, technically men at that point, I guess, but their actions suggested their brains hadn't caught up to their age bracket.

My first fall on campus, I began sleeping with a boy named Chad. In my head I was dating him, but it seems inaccurate to label it that way seeing as how only one of us thought that. Chad was six foot two, really handsome, and super popular. He was one of about ten of us from our floor that regularly hung out together. I was so grateful to have found a group, to have been accepted into the popular crowd, and, in my mind, to be the object of someone's affection. In all reality, it was likely just a relationship of proximity. My roommate was seeing Chad's friend, who also lived on our floor, and since the group of us were always together, it was convenient for me to be "seeing" Chad too.

I let Chad treat me like shit.

We slept together off and on for the better part of a year and a half. It was a convenient arrangement for him. The only thing I got from it was another hit to my self-esteem.

*   *   *

At the end-of-year picnic, everyone living on my floor in Akers Hall voted on their own superlatives. I won in three categories: "Prettiest

Eyes," "Best Chest," and "Most Fun at Parties." I probably should have been embarrassed that my eyes, my boobs, and my boozing were my legacy those first two years in college, but I wasn't. Quite the contrary, actually. I was *proud* to be that loved. That's how I saw it. How could you be the most fun at parties unless everyone loved you? My definition of love revolved around being noticed, being popular, being memorable. I *was* fun, and we all had a blast together. It felt like some weird college way for my dormmates to honor that.

As it became more and more clear that I was not Chad's girlfriend, but his friend with benefits, I took my drunken affections elsewhere. One night during my second year, I got so drunk at a dorm-room party that I snuck across the hall and wrote crazy love notes to a new boy who had just moved in. I didn't remember writing the notes, but the new boy did.

Dan Zamboni was so flattered by my approach that he walked down the hall the next morning and asked me out. We went on our first date that very afternoon. Dan was not a Chad. We dated, officially, not just in my head, for the better part of eighteen months. This was my first good relationship in college, one where the guy wasn't cheating on me or in love with their former girlfriend. Dan was also not a big drinker, my typical type. He was a bodybuilder, a serious one, and he would spend two to three hours a day working out. He took his body seriously, which was more than fine with me, and it paid off. He actually won several bodybuilding competitions.

The only problem with Dan was me. I was a hot mess. After moving out of the dorm into my own apartment, my partying only intensified. With more freedom came more opportunity. I continued drinking heavily despite Dan's healthier ways, and I would call him regularly at 2 a.m. wasted. I would go out partying and when I some-how made it back to my apartment, I'd get sad, and lonely, and I'd call Dan. Sometimes I'd cry on the phone with him until I passed out. He hated it. And that should have been enough to end our relationship, but it wasn't.

Dan complained about his grades all the time. He was in the engineering program taking a rigorous load of classes. I couldn't understand why he wouldn't just cut back on going to the gym to study. The complaining was a trigger for me, and ultimately, an easy excuse. Having been raised in a house where my mother constantly whined about my father's behavior but never did anything about it, my tolerance for complaints without action was incredibly low. So low, in fact, that I tanked our relationship because of it. I convinced myself that I didn't want to be with someone that failed out of college, even if he was a hot bodybuilder, so I broke up with him. In reality, I probably knew that a break up was imminent. The strain of me living in an apartment and partying all the time was obvious, but I wasn't going to let Dan break up with me, so I ended it before he could.

It was stupid. And wholly indicative of how I handled relation-ships with men. I didn't trust that men would be good to me, or maybe I didn't trust that there were good men. I looked for any and every indication that they would live up to my low expectations and then used that to create distance between us. I had experienced enough hurt as a child, so I sabotaged anything that felt remotely good before it had a chance to turn bad.

Dan was kind, hard working, and good to me. I didn't deserve him then, but it had nothing to do with my history of sexual assault.

A year later, I tried to get back together with Dan. He didn't want anything to do with me. Served me right, didn't it?

* * *

Discovering what I wanted to do for a living actually took some real effort. I changed my major a bunch of times, from nursing, to premed, to international relations, to broadcasting, and then, finally, the one that stuck, advertising. I always found something wrong with the other career pursuits, but advertising was different. I was good at it; that creative spark and fast-paced energy matched my need for speed and adventure. I joined the advertising club at Michigan State and quickly signed up to go on a trip to Chicago to tour one of the big-time ad agencies. It was on this trip that I met Skylar.

The word *club* makes this sound like something casual, but those of us that regularly participated took it quite seriously and competed in several advertising competitions. The advertising club as a whole was pretty big, so we were split into smaller teams for the purpose of competing. On my team there were two guys, Skylar, myself, and one other girl. These competitions were a big deal at the national level, with Fortune 500 companies like Nestle sponsoring them. We would start with epic brainstorming sessions where we just riffed ideas off of each other. But those sessions quickly morphed into late nights chugging coffee while we collectively prepared for the competition. Because of all the time we spent together, we formed an incredibly close bond, both personally and socially. We even had a nickname for our group, "The Ad Gang." When we beat out the five other groups in our advertising class to win the pitch competition for our mock client, we all got to go to Chicago together for the regional competition. The second I got on stage in Chicago, I fell in love. I was a natural presenter, and the rush of adrenaline and attention was almost as intoxicating as the alcohol at the bars afterwards. I ended up coming in second place for Best Presenter.

Skylar was also a drinker and a party girl, but there was more to it than that. We just clicked. Our time in Chicago together sealed the deal, and we were pretty inseparable after that. When The Ad Gang ended up going to nationals in Los Angeles, all of us were stoked! The Annual Addy Awards were a big deal, and we were wowed by the opportunity to hob knob with all of the big wig advertising executives at exclusive private events. We felt like we were watching our future selves.

We ended up coming in tenth in the competition, which we were pretty proud of considering our motto was "Work hard. Play harder." We wanted to celebrate. So after the final event, the five of us went to the bar together. Eventually the others faded away, heading back to the hotel to get some sleep. But not Skylar and I. We were just getting warmed up! We stayed out all night, drinking and doing cocaine with two boys we met at the bar. It was dumb, and only the second time in my life I ever did cocaine, but it was LA, so it felt like the thing to do.

This was classic Darlene back then, ready to chase the party, the excitement, the energy. It wasn't the coke that made me feel like I could fly; it was being the life of the party, surrounded by people who seemingly wanted to be with me as much as I wanted to be with them. That was my elixir, the thing that quieted the voice in my head that told me I was dirty and tainted and undeserving of love or attention.

When we came back to the hotel the next morning, our club manager was livid. Skylar and I held back giggles as we stood there and took our tongue lashing. The night was epic, and if this was the punishment for having that much fun, it was totally worth it.

About the time I met Skylar, I was really struggling in my relationships with my current roommates. Four of us from Akers Hall had moved into an apartment together, and things weren't going well. They did not appreciate my constant partying, and didn't understand my sometimes erratic behavior, leading them to belittle or ignore instead of support me.

Our apartment was on the first floor of the complex. Down the hall was the laundry room. One night, I carried my laundry basket down the hall to do my laundry, leaving the door to our apartment open. We always did that, left the apartment door open when we went to do laundry. I don't know why. As I was bent over throwing my clothes in the washing machine from my laundry basket, all of a sudden, the hairs on the back of my neck stood up. Like it was a horror film, I slowly turned around and there was a man in a hooded sweatshirt standing directly behind me in the doorway. I went stiff, my body reverting to the same survival tactic like every time I was raped. The guy was right there, literally an arms length away from me. He reached out and grabbed my boob, and somehow that broke the spell. I screamed. As loud and panicked as I could. I screamed so loud my roommates heard me through the open door and came running which scared the guy off. We called the police. When the police investigated, they found footprints outside our apartment, and surmised that the guy had been watching us through a crack in the curtain covering our sliding glass door.

Despite what the police said, my roommates didn't believe me. They heard me scream, but never saw the guy. They thought I had concocted this attack by a random hooded assailant for attention. The eye rolls and side bar comments added to the retraumatization of the situation. I started drinking even more after that. I never wanted to be alone, and now, I didn't even want to be in my own house.

So, I spent most of my time at Skylar's.

Skylar lived in a big house with another girlfriend and four guys, so not only was there space for me, but I felt safe there because someone was always at home. When I told her about the incident with the guy in the laundry room, I completely freaked out, shaking and crying as if he'd done more than just touch my breast. Skylar was sympathetic, but confused, so I told her. I finally let what happened to me slip out of the box and out of my mouth into someone else's ears. It was the first time I had told anyone but Pete.

"You gotta tell your parents, Dar," Skylar said emphatically.

But I was adamant. I had kept the secret that long. What good would it do to tell them now?

Skylar persisted. "Look, if you're not going to tell your parents, at least go talk to someone. There's counselors at school that would have to keep it private, but at least then you wouldn't be carrying it all on your own."

I was incredibly skeptical, but I was also tired. Tired of what this secret was doing to my insides and the way it was leaking out into my life no matter what I did to stop it. "Okay," I agreed. "I'll look into it."

And I did. I made an appointment with the on-campus psychiatry team at Michigan State. But this was the mid-eighties and psychiatrists, especially on college campuses, were all old white men that pushed drugs hard. I didn't need more drugs, I had enough of those. I kept going for a while, but I hated it. Even better than therapy, though, was the realization that I could tell someone, even if it wasn't my parents. And when I told, that someone might actually believe me, listen to me, and try to help me.

Skylar graduated in 1988 and moved away, and I once again found myself alone.

*　　*　　*

As crazy as it sounds, I was never worried about my drinking. I wasn't addicted to the alcohol. I was addicted to being the party girl. I couldn't quit the people, the fun, the sense of belonging.

So, anxious to make friends and in need of money as I was burning through my summer savings quickly, I took a job as a waitress at a nice Italian restaurant, Coscarelli's, in East Lansing. The staff at Coscarelli's lived the industry life—working late, partying later, sleeping until we had to be in class or at the restaurant, and doing it all over again the next day. At one after party, I met another waitress named Danielle, Dani for short. Like Skylar, Dani liked to drink, and she liked to party. We were instant best friends.

Dani introduced me to her other friend, Bethany, a woman who could stop traffic with her good looks, but was fully committed to her high school boyfriend. We drank together and partied together. We were on top of the world. We even came up with our own saying of solidarity—*"Here's to the men that we love. Here's to the men that love us. If the men that we love, don't love us, then fuck 'em, and here's to us!"* We sealed the commitment with a little dance, a high five, and a lot of laughter. Nothing could touch us.

The three of us eventually moved in together. We felt like such adults. Bethany had a job working for the State of Michigan in telecommunications, Danielle was finishing school at Michigan State, and I had recently graduated and gotten a job as a marketing assistant at Capital One Federal Savings Bank. Every morning, I would read the headlines from the local newspaper, *The Lansing State Journal*, out loud while the three of us ate breakfast before going off to our respective jobs. It was such a magical time.

But my demons would still surface on occasion. I started getting angry when I drank. Not every time, but enough that it became a problem. I often couldn't remember what it was that set me off. We were all out drinking at a bar one night, and for some unknown reason, I got super pissed with Dani. To this day, I don't know why. We were in the girls bathroom, and I just started screaming at her. "You're such a horrible person! Why do you have to be such a stupid bitch? I hate you!" Vile, nasty things spewed out of my mouth as I spit them at her with a vengeance I could feel but couldn't understand. Eventually, the altercation got physical and Bethany had to step in to break it up.

The next morning, I asked Dani if I could talk to her. She graciously agreed, which is more than I might have done if the situation was reversed. Given this opportunity to repair our friendship, I felt like I had to offer a real explanation, not just a bullshit apology.

"Look, Dani, I don't even know what to say. I'm so very sorry. I don't know how to say this, but I . . . I . . . need to tell you something that may help explain why I acted that way." I told her about my rapes. I explained that something in the bar triggered me, and I took it out on her. The words I screamed in her face were the words I wished I'd had the courage to hurl at my brothers when they hurt me.

"I know I was horrible to you, and it's a lot to ask, but I hope you can forgive me. I love you and our friendship, and I don't want to lose that," I said, tears running down my face.

"Jesus, Darlene! Forget about the stupid fight. I'm so sorry that happened to you. Of course I forgive you." Then she gave me a giant hug.

I didn't feel worthy of her forgiveness or her friendship in that moment, but I was so thankful that she didn't disown me, that she didn't give up on me and throw me away.

Dani wanted me to start seeing someone again, maybe give the psych team at Michigan State another try. But by that point, my therapy was alcohol and being around as many people as I could. I figured I could out-fun my hurt.

And then I met Wade.

*　*　*

After college, I basically gave up on men. I wasn't great at picking them to begin with, and when I did pick a good one, I would find something wrong with him. So, I convinced myself that I could only count on my girlfriends, and I would just stick with having fun with them.

Famous last words.

It was fall of 1990, Michigan State's Homecoming weekend. By this point, Dani's boyfriend had moved down to the Detroit area, so she was often there visiting him. She called me one morning after a party at her boyfriend's brother's house. They were all eating breakfast when one of them mentioned having an extra ticket to the Homecoming game. Dani thought I might like to go . . . with one catch. According to her, there was a guy there, her boyfriend's brother's best friend, that she thought I'd like to meet. Dani couched it as "He's funny and good looking, but not my type." Apparently, Dani's boyfriend told Wade, "Darlene's cute, but she's a little on the heavy side." Not exactly glowing endorsements on either end, but we both somehow said yes, and the plan was hatched.

We all met up at the tailgate and proceeded to preparty with the other thousands of MSU students and fans taking up residence in the parking lots outside the stadium. At first, there wasn't much interaction between Wade and me with all of the noise and people in the background, but it was obvious we both felt like the other exceeded initial expectations. Wade *was* funny, and he liked to drink, so naturally we hit it off. He gave me cinnamon schnapps in a Dixie cup, and we saw each other every day after that.

Wade was a blue collar, down-home farm boy. Given that background, I thought he would be a hard worker and practical, that "salt of the earth" kind of guy. He was also extremely close to his family, including his nieces and nephews, and that felt important to me. Even though he often embarrassed me when he was drunk, I was already ashamed of myself so it felt like a small price to pay. At least at that point.

We dated for about six months before I broke up with Wade. In January, I had decided to move back in with Mom and Dad now that Bethany was married and Dani was off doing her own thing. It seemed silly to spend the money on an apartment just for me, and my parents had moved from our blue saltbox house in Port Huron to a house they built on the lake, a house I had no history with. My job at the bank was going really well, and I thoroughly enjoyed marketing, but I was twenty-four and living in my parents' house, and I felt alone in an entirely new way.

Wade and I had stayed friends after the break up and would occasionally hang out, but casually. In April, I got offered a regional marketing manager position in Springfield, Missouri. When I told Wade I was moving, he asked if we could get together before I left. We went to an art festival in East Lansing with a collective group of friends where the alcohol started flowing at 10 a.m. After drinking all day, while sitting at the bar at Olga's Kitchen, we somehow professed our undying love for each other. Fueled by the moment, Wade proposed. I said yes. And then he went to the bathroom to throw up.

Perhaps that should have been a sign.

The next morning, with raging hangovers, we discussed the matter. Still not in our right minds, but neither of us having the balls to state the obvious, we agreed to move forward with the marriage plans.

Not a month later, my dad had a massive heart attack.

I had been working my new job for just two weeks, but flights back home were really cheap then, and I wanted to come back for our annual Memorial Day weekend lake party. My dad would go back to Port Huron once a month on a Friday to balance the books for my mom's Christian bookstore, spend the night at the Marysville condo they still owned, and then head back home on Saturday morning. This was the plan for Memorial Day weekend. We finished setting up for the party and Dad still hadn't arrived. Everyone started arriving and I started to get nervous. An hour passed, then two, and finally, the phone rang. I picked up to hear a police officer on the other end. Immediately, my heart started racing and tears pricked my eyes. Apparently, my dad had started experiencing symptoms of a heart attack on his drive from Port Huron to Brooklyn. Ever the pragmatist, he figured if he could just make it to the University of Michigan hospital in Ann Arbor, about halfway between the two, he would get the best care. Despite having to pull over several times to vomit, he not only made it, but parked his own car and walked himself into the ER. He was, in fact, having a massive heart attack

I was distraught. All I could think was, *How can I possibly go back to Missouri now?*

After my father's heart attack, the guilt I felt was paralyzing. Once I left home for Michigan State, I rarely went back. For holidays, yes, and I worked all summer at the local country club in Port Huron, but I never went home on weekends or just to visit. It wasn't like I was worried about being assaulted by David or Don. By the time I went to Michigan State, David was married with three kids, and Don had inherited his own family. At the holidays, our interactions were brief, and we were never alone in the house together.

So, I wasn't intentionally avoiding the danger at home. There was just nothing there for me.

I didn't want to sit at the same dinner table with David and Don and be forced to put a smile on my face, to act like it was no big deal, to pretend we were the one big happy family Mom and Dad believed us to be.

I didn't want to fake it anymore.

But, after Dad had his heart attack, I realized that pretending was going to be a permanent part of my life. If I wanted to be a good daughter to him, to Mom, that was part of the deal.

And Wade? Well, Wade was my tether to Michigan. If my dad hadn't had a heart attack, I don't know if I would have gone through with the wedding, but the idea of my dad dying and my mom being left alone was too much for me. I had sacrificed my truth to keep that part of my family together, and I couldn't bear the thought of pursuing a life somewhere else while one of them was suffering.

It wasn't my responsibility to take care of them, but I couldn't imagine any of my siblings doing it the way I would. That need to always be in control superseded my desire to build my own life away from them.

So, I said "Yes," and I stuck with it.

2005. My children Jake, Sierra, and Austin
at Chicago's Navy Pier.

8
1992–2013

A woman will do anything and everything to make a relationship work.
That's why she almost never regrets when it's time to walk away.
—UNKNOWN

I married Wade on August 8, 1992.

I stared at the minister while I recited my vows, making eye contact, intently parroting his words when prompted. He kept jerking his head to his left, toward Wade. At the time, I couldn't tell if he had a tic of some sort or if he was trying to ward off an insect attack, but later, it dawned on me that he was trying to get me to profess my vows not to him, but to my soon-to-be husband. Perhaps that should have been a sign.

Of course, there were many signs leading up to the big day, including when Wade left his wallet in our hotel room and someone stole all of our money. And when the bridal party frantically asked for my engagement ring so there was something to exchange during the ceremony because Wade left my wedding ring in the glove compartment of his Bronco. But, most telling was how I felt. And why.

I felt on top of the world on my wedding day, surrounded by family and friends. Wade was from a small town with a huge farm family, so between that and all of those attending from my side, over four hundred people came out to celebrate the occasion. I was enamored with the attention—the hugs and kisses and fawning over the bride. All of these people showing up to support me must be proof that I was loved. Proof that I wasn't dirty, undeserving, or permanently tainted. Proof that my past would have no bearing on my future. I floated through the night, somewhat immune to the chaos of Wade's blunders, and when I got to the point where I said, "I do," there was no hesitation. I didn't say it because I was *in* love, though. Love was an emotion I had been taught to doubt, to mistrust. No, I said it out of obligation . . . out of a belief that this was the best I was going to get. Wade was a nice enough guy, and he was funny and attractive. We genuinely had a good time together. I thought that was probably enough, maybe all I deserved. And marrying Wade meant I would never be alone again, which mattered almost more than anything else.

After graduating college, getting married felt like the thing to do. It was the early '90s and still typical for women to get married in their early twenties. I felt like every weekend held another friend's shower or wedding, and at twenty-six, I was feeling the pressure. The control freak that haunted my brain was constantly hammering home the rules we'd agreed to: *Come on Darlene, you don't want to be some old lady. Settle down already.* I wanted to be married before I was thirty and done having my kids by thirty-five.

My sister Diane hadn't met her husband until later in life and watching her struggle with having young kids in her forties made a strong impression on me. I didn't want that for my life. I wanted to enjoy my retirement years kid-free, and in my head, that meant I had to get a move on. Marrying Wade put me back on track.

To be fair, I gave him an out. Given his rather impromptu proposal, he hadn't acquired a ring before asking, so we went shopping for one together after agreeing to move forward with the engagement. Something about looking for rings made it real for me. This man was going to be my husband, and he didn't know. How could I keep such a profound secret from my own husband?

I felt like I owed it to Wade to tell him about my abuse *before* we got married. In case he wanted to change his mind.

But how do you just introduce that kind of information into a relationship, particularly one that had gotten this far? I started by telling Wade that there was something he should know before committing to me. That I was dirty and cheap and shouldn't be married, didn't deserve to be married because of it. When I finally told Wade what happened to me, he didn't break off the engagement. Instead, he said, "Darlene, you know I'm not going to leave you. I love you." And he never brought it up again. Done deal.

It's what I wanted to hear, I think, but I'm not sure Wade ever understood the magnitude of what I shared with him. How deeply the information he now possessed directed my life and how much I was not "over it" despite the fact that I continued to act the part in front of my brothers and family. My constant need for control in every situation, the must-win attitude that pervaded our marriage, they started here. This was the origin story.

It's telling that I chose to only have two of my siblings in my wedding party—Diane and Dale. I wonder now what Don and David thought about that snub. Did they see it as such or were they grateful to get out of wedding duties? I may not have been deeply in love with Wade, may not have even understood what love actually was, but I was very clear on what it was not. And I didn't want any of that standing behind me on my wedding day.

*   *   *

Our first year of marriage was anything but an extended honeymoon.

While we were engaged, I kept my job in Missouri, perhaps somehow intuiting that I would need to be the breadwinner, while Wade remained in Michigan. As newlyweds, though, this seemed like a horrible way to build a marriage. Something had to change. Wade's boss found him a job, but it was three hours from Springfield, so we moved to the small town of Warsaw, Missouri, and each drove an hour and a half one way back and forth to work. When we did see each other during the week, we were exhausted, and on the weekends, there was nothing to do in Warsaw. We had no friends, no family, no nothing close by. We were both miserable.

After a year and a half, I just couldn't take it anymore, so I suggested we move back to Michigan. I sought out a job at an advertising agency in Kalamazoo. Wade took a job at a factory working third shift and weekends. Once again, he was never home. The whole point of getting married was so I would *never* be alone, but Wade kept taking jobs that gave him less and less time with me. It was a constant fight between us.

"Wade, you have a college degree. Why are you taking these shift jobs that are the total opposite of my schedule?"

He'd throw back, "Because that's all I can get."

"Bullshit," I'd counter. "You have a degree that you aren't even trying to use. Why?"

Knowing I was frustrated, Wade suggested that his job could be buying fixer-uppers and doing the work himself to remodel and then flip them. He was good with his hands and had the ability to do the work, and I was desperate for him to find and stick with something productive that was close to home, so I finally agreed to buy a real work-in-progress as our first home in Kalamazoo.

Eventually, I got laid off, a common occurrence in the advertising industry. I knew I wanted to start having kids soon and it was becoming clear that Wade was not going to be a reliable provider, so I needed to find a job that was stable in an industry where I could climb. Fast.

In 1995, I landed a job as the marketing director of an ATM network, Magic Line, Inc., based in Dearborn, Michigan, just north of Detroit. At the time, Magic Line was the only electronic funds transfer company in Michigan. At just twenty-nine years old, I was running the entire marketing department. I doubled my salary, inherited a staff of four people, and for the first time saw the potential for personal growth that was possible for me if I just absolutely killed it.

At the same time, Wade still didn't have a job, still hadn't finished the renovations on our house in Kalamazoo, and had no concept of the work I was putting in to set us up for financial success.

We moved to Beverly Hills, a suburb of Detroit, five houses down from Lulu, my best friend from high school, and her husband.

By that point, I was already fed up. I found myself becoming attracted to other men, including one who I would regularly kiss at parties when Wade wasn't there until I got called out by my friends for my behavior. It wasn't an affair, per se, as all we did was kiss, but it was a flashing red-warning sign that the trouble in our marriage was getting worse, not better.

One night about a year after we had moved to the neighborhood, we were over at Lulu's house hanging out with her and her husband in their basement. True Midwesterners, we were deeply engrossed in a heated game of Euchre. Wade had been picking at me all night, well, for months really, little remarks but in a tone that was all too familiar. When I made a move in the game that Wade didn't like, he went after me again.

"That was a stupid move! Why did you play that card?" he said, snidely.

It was a small jab, but it was said with the same condescending voice my brothers would use on me when we would play cards as kids. It was the last straw, and I whipped back at him, "Fuck you, Wade. I am so done with you. So done with this marriage. I'm out!" I got up and walked back to our house, thinking about how fast I could divorce him as my feet covered the distance between their house and ours.

The heat of the night's exchange wore off, and I didn't take any action at the time. I was busy with my new job, and Wade was excellent at making up, but I had it in the back of my head that the marriage was headed for the dumpster.

And then I got pregnant.

*   *   *

At the time, Wade had finally gotten a job working for an agricultural company. But, again, it was a ninety-minute drive, and he had to leave at 3 a.m. The only way we managed to get pregnant is because we went on a camping trip with a bunch of folks from Michigan State and had sex in the tent. Apparently, that tent has a long history of producing offspring from these camping trips. To be fair, I had gone off of birth control intentionally about nine months after Wade convinced me not to leave him. I was twenty-nine years old and decided if I was going to stay with him, it was time to start having babies.

Our daughter Sierra was born April 30, 1997. The delivery was fast and furious which meant no epidural for me and a host of complications. The recovery was hard, but being at home with an infant, and a husband who worked an hour and a half away and had to leave in the middle of the night to get there, was even worse. I may not have been enamored with him at the time, but I needed Wade's help, especially if I was going to keep rising in my own career.

Knowing how hard it was on me to have Wade gone all the time, Lulu and her husband introduced him to their good friend who owned a construction company. He hired Wade to be a manager for him. Finally, Wade had a job during normal working hours that was near our house. Unfortunately, it didn't go as smoothly as I would have hoped. Wade complained constantly that nobody there knew anything and they were always in his business. A year into the job, he just walked out. He quit without telling me or his boss. Imagine the embarrassment. Here, we've asked my best friend and her husband to vouch for Wade with a friend of theirs and he just up and quits.

No attempt to reconcile the issues. No formal resignation. He always thought he was in the right, and there was no point arguing with him, although I certainly tried.

It seems insane to me now that I stayed. Except, I had a baby and a high-stakes job and the self-imposed expectation that this was the bed I made and therefore I had to lie in it.

And, I wanted more children. I didn't want Sierra to be an only child. For whatever reason, my perception at the time was that it was a cruel thing to do to a kid. Maybe it had something to do with my never wanting to be alone. I didn't want my child to ever feel like she was alone. So, I got pregnant again in September 2000, but I had a miscarriage sitting on the toilet at work sometime in the first four to six weeks.

We were supposed to wait three months to try again, but we didn't. I got pregnant two months later, with not one, but two babies. Twins. I honestly wasn't that surprised as we have sets of twins on both sides of my family. The prospect of having them didn't scare me, but it did feel like I had sealed my fate with Wade. Conceptually, I could imagine being a single mother of two children, but three? It felt like God, the Universe, Destiny, whatever you want to call it was telling me that choices have consequences, and mine was to stay in a miserable marriage with a man I couldn't count on. And now, I had to figure out how to take care of myself and my family all on my own.

The company I was working for at the time was about to go bankrupt. Wade had finally found a job working for a custom-build cabinet company, but knowing his history with employment, I must not have trusted that he could support us, because I fortuitously signed up for an Aflac policy. Thank goodness I did, because one day, Wade walked in and unceremoniously told me he quit his job. He knew I was pregnant, and he knew my company was not doing well, but he just quit. Same explanation: "I just can't handle that guy anymore. My boss doesn't know what he's doing."

Two weeks later, my company went under, and we all lost our jobs. While incredibly grateful for Aflac and my remaining commissions, Aflac was not meant to pay for the life of a family of five. I knew I had to find another job, and I diligently looked from May to September, but to say that companies were reticent to hire a woman pregnant with twins with another child at home was an understatement. I finally landed a job in September but because I was still on maternity leave, I didn't start until the beginning of December. But it was a blessing in disguise to have those months off to dedicate to my growing family.

As December approached, I started to panic a bit about what I was going to do with three young children when I went back to work. Wade couldn't handle being a stay-at-home dad, and none of our family was in a position to help. The woman who lived across the street from us at the time had two young children herself. She and her husband were the sweetest family, and they didn't have much money, so when we asked if she would be interested in working as our nanny, it really turned into the perfect situation for everyone. She would watch the twins while Sierra and her girls were at school and then keep an eye on everyone while she prepared our dinner for us. I don't know what I would have done without her, but it was also a constant reminder of how incapable Wade was of being anything other than my fourth child.

*　*　*

As much as being a mother mattered to me, so did cultivating a thriving career for myself. I needed to support my family, yes, but I was also determined to be successful. I refused to let my brothers win, to succumb to the pain and trauma of what they had done to me. To me, winning meant making money, holding positions with hefty titles, and being loved by coworkers and bosses throughout. I had a vision of where I wanted to go and who I wanted to be. I simply would not allow myself to fail.

In the late nineties, I had essentially capped out my salary in marketing at my job at Magic Line. I knew if I wanted to keep climbing, I would have to make a potentially risky move. Sales had never been something I considered before. The uncertainty of making a base salary but relying on commissions to bring in the real money seemed daunting, particularly when Wade was so unreliable. But, I decided I just had to make things happen for myself. I took a sales executive job and a $30,000 pay cut. It was one of the scariest moments of my life, but that calculated risk paid off. Trusting myself, my own aptitude, and my own ability paid off.

I realized that I could keep increasing my salary and my commissions if I moved positions every five to six years. Changing companies also meant expanding the products and solutions I could sell, and the more options I had to present to clients, the more likely I was to close the sale. In college, I was addicted to the party, the fun, the energy, the people. It was no different in my career. I became addicted to the sale, the feeling of closing the deal, the relationship building required to get people to trust me enough to buy from me. From then on, I was always top three in sales or account management. I just wouldn't accept anything less.

As the summer of 2000 approached, we decided to get out of the city. Wade was never much of a city boy, and he had done his time in Detroit for me, so now it was his turn. We bought a hundred-year-old fixer-upper farmhouse on three acres in Delton, Michigan. As one might expect, the pace of life there was different, and so were the wives. They wanted to drink beer and sit at bonfires while their kids played in the fields. That's not the type of woman I had become, but it was the type of man I had married. Wade was in his element, but I was floundering. I started driving to Junior League meetings in Kalamazoo and Grand Rapids, each over a half hour away, trying to build community with other women like me. It was a difficult time for me. I felt so alone with no close girlfriends around. I didn't resent Wade for the move, but my sadness began to overwhelm me.

Wade often said that I never talked about the abuse while we were married, and he's right. I was busy raising little kids. Building a career and mothering and trying to live copacetically with him occupied all of my mental energy and my time. There was no space to address the secret I buried in my box. I was absorbed in taking care of my own kids and building a beautiful life for them.

Plus, I wasn't worried about my brothers at that point in my life; I knew I was safe. With all our moves, we were anywhere from four to eight hours away from the rest of my family, and we only saw them once or twice a year. We weren't close physically, and we certainly weren't close emotionally. It was almost as if they didn't exist . . . almost.

* * *

I hated the person I was becoming being married to Wade. We never operated as partners, but the higher I rose on the corporate ladder, the more I believed he saw me as his cash cow. Wade often retorted that he was "sacrificing everything for my career," but I never felt like I had any other choice. It was never an option to decide if I wanted to be a stay-at-home mom because Wade could never hold down a job long enough for us to be financially secure. Even though I was better suited to being a working parent, I resented that I never had the chance to choose. I resented that I felt so alone in being the only one responsible for our family.

It was one of several things I grew to resent in our marriage. Wade's drinking was another. Nearly every time we were out with friends, he got hammered. Not during the day, necessarily, and not while taking care of our kids, but he had no off button at social gatherings. Once he started, he was headed straight to drunk. And when he was drinking, he was an asshole. At least to me.

Early on in our marriage, we were at a Barenaked Ladies concert with some of our friends. Wade was getting a little out of control, so I discreetly asked him if he could please tone down the drinking. Instead of responding to me in kind, he started screaming at the top of his lungs. "Fuck you! I'll do what I want!" Mortified, I tried to get him to quiet down. Thank God the concert was loud as it drowned out some of the yelling, but it did little to cover my embarrassment.

On another occasion when we were living in Kalamazoo, Wade and I went to my company Christmas party. An open bar is a dangerous siren for Wade, and it called to him all night. When it was time to go home, I told Wade I was going to drive, but he refused to give me the keys. I stood outside the car arguing with him but finally relented when other people from the party started coming out to the parking lot. Wade started driving like he was insane, flying around turns and going way too fast. I was terrified and started screaming for him to let me out of the car. He ignored me. I finally yelled that he either needed to stop the car, or I was going to open the door. That got his attention, and he slid to a stop. I got out of the car and started walking. He kept trying to convince me to get back in, but I refused. Eventually, his bravado fading with his buzz, he got out of the car and handed me the keys.

I hated that Wade couldn't handle his booze. It's not like I had become a teetotaler, but I had grown out of the wasted-or-nothing mentality. I wanted us to be able to enjoy a couple of drinks with friends or colleagues together, but that wasn't possible. When I started working in leadership positions, I stopped inviting Wade to any of my company events. He couldn't hold a business conversation, he always drank too much, and he inevitably embarrassed me. I wanted to be with a man who could impress my coworkers, not annoy them.

So, when I met Scott Babcock in 2002, I was instantly impressed by his aptitude and his presence. Scott owned an ATM signage company that partnered with the company I was working for at the time. Through that partnership, I became Scott's top salesperson. We interacted often and developed a mutual respect for each other's talents. We were friends, yes, but that was all. Until it wasn't.

Over time, Scott and I became attracted to each other. In my mind, he was exactly the type of man I should have been with—successful, good looking, smart, fun, but in control. My twins were two years old at the time, and I had about had it with Wade. I wanted something for me. A man that saw and appreciated my aptitude and had his own ambition. I started seeing Scott romantically in December 2004.

In January 2005, I filed for divorce from Wade. We told the entire family, and the divorce was supposed to be final in August of that year. That same month, I agreed to fly with Wade to Evanston, Illinois, to meet with a marriage counselor, Rich Nisbet. I was hesitant because I was seriously done with this man, but some friends of ours encouraged us to go even if we ultimately decided to end the marriage to help ensure a smoother separation, especially with the kids. I continued the relationship with Scott during this time, although we only saw each other in person three or four times because he lived in Utah, and we were still living in Michigan.

I did not want to let go of my relationship with Scott. Looking back, I think I started the relationship subconsciously hoping that if I cheated on Wade, he would finally let me leave. But as luck would have it, I fell in love with Scott, what I believed to be the real kind, but Scott was also married. Our therapist was unequivocal in his lack of support for this relationship. As he said, "You may be getting a divorce, but he is not, and it is unethical for you to be seeing a married man." In May, I called Scott and ended the relationship. It was heart breaking for me at the time, but he agreed it was the right thing to do. I didn't want to stay in my marriage, but I was raised to believe kids deserved a two-parent home, and practically, what was I going to do as the single mother of three young kids? My resolve faltered, and Wade succeeded at persuading me to stay.

*   *   *

I don't know how much it helped our marriage, but I ended up seeing our therapist, Rich, on my own thereafter. I liked the techniques he used with Wade and me to help us better communicate and survive our marriage, and I thought he might be able to help me apply those same techniques to my own trauma. In August 2005, we moved to Evanston, Illinois, an insanely expensive suburb of Chicago. I needed to get back to city life if I had any hope of salvaging this marriage, so I convinced my company to let me take over their largest client who was headquartered in Chicago. Once we moved to Evanston, Rich's office was two blocks from the house we ultimately purchased. I started going to see him during my lunch break. His approach was intense, guiding me to relive my sexual assaults through visual images, confronting and talking about it openly and directly to help me release it. I was skeptical at first, but I couldn't argue with the results. My persistent nightmares started dying down, and I was no longer so insanely afraid of being alone.

From November 2005 until Rich moved in 2008, I saw him every single day during the week. Wade knew that I was going to therapy with Rich, knew that it was a daily occurrence, knew that it was for the trauma associated with my childhood sexual assaults. He never really asked me how it was going, and I never volunteered any update unless he asked. He must have known it was helping since the nightmares finally stopped, but if he was otherwise curious, he never let on. It's such a salient example to me of how little Wade and I actually communicated during that time. We were already living parallel lives inside of our marriage.

* * *

It took another seven years for me to finally cut the cord.

In 2008, we were still living in Evanston. True to form, Wade didn't have a job and was supposed to be remodeling the two-flat home we had purchased in Evanston. When the market crashed, we lost hundreds of thousands of dollars in equity overnight. Our house that was supposed to be such a good investment was now worth half of what we paid for it.

At about the same time, I was offered a promotion to the role of national sales manager, again with a significant increase in pay. The only caveat was that it had to be based in the Southeast, so I was flying back and forth from Evanston. It made no sense to keep doing that once our investment tanked, especially since we could get three times the house for half the price in the Southeast. We just needed to get out and move on. So, we did a short sale on the house in Evanston and allowed our house in Michigan, another of Wade's fixer-uppers, to be foreclosed on. With our credit in shambles, we moved to North Carolina, knowing we'd have to rent for the first several years before we could rebuild.

At first, that seemed like a real inconvenience because we had always owned our homes, but we moved into a fantastic neighborhood and made friends quickly. The house we rented was bigger than anything we had ever lived in before, a gorgeous three-story home that I desperately wanted to furnish with beautiful things. Unfortunately, though, we had sunk all of our money into buying homes, and with our credit destroyed, the best I could do was to buy used or rent-to-own from the couple who owned the home. It was embarrassing, but the house was so perfect for hosting that we made the best out of it. In fact, we ended up hosting Thanksgiving for the neighborhood three years in a row.

In 2011, my parents were in town for the Thanksgiving holiday. While I prepared to host forty people for the holiday feast, Wade was getting wasted. His liquor of choice that night? Straight scotch. By the time we finished dinner, I was already irritated, but when I walked in to clean up and saw that the dark cherry wood table where we had just eaten dinner was covered in scotch, I was livid. My two best girlfriends jumped into action, assigning the other neighbors to dish duty and putting leftovers in Tupperware.

"Oh my God. I'm so mortified," I whispered to one of them. "I can't believe this. My beautiful table." I was near tears.

In a hushed voice so as not to be overheard, she tried to make me feel better. "Don't worry about it, honey. We'll clean it up together."

But, I couldn't stop apologizing. As the host, it was incredibly embarrassing that your own husband was the one that created such a mess. The night probably would have ended there, but we had an after-dinner tradition. An all-ages game of 7 Up 7 Down, so while everyone started setting up the tables for the game, I went to find Wade.

I checked our bedroom and the bathrooms, thinking maybe he had gotten sick, but then I saw a glow from the doors leading out to the back deck. I found Wade on our *wooden* deck, where he had decided it would be a good idea to set up our fire pit. With the fire going, he added music, the makings of a real party. He was clearly in the mood for dancing because by the time I walked out there, he was locked in a Patrick Swayze move with the neighbor who was rumored to be sleeping with some of the husbands. I couldn't believe it. I turned to look back in the house and saw my parents staring straight at Wade and his dance partner. They had a perfect view of his dirty dancing. I felt the shame creep up my neck. And the rage.

It was one thing to humiliate me in front of our friends, but in front of my parents? I had spent my entire life trying to protect my parents from embarrassment and shame, and my own husband was now the source of both.

At that point, I was done with being mortified. In fact, I was done . . . period. I told Wade that night that I was divorcing him.

It took until March of the following year to go through the mediators we hired to prepare the formal separation paperwork. Not wanting to disrupt the kids while they were in school, we didn't tell them until June of that year. In the state of North Carolina, you have to be separated for a year before the divorce can be final, so Wade and I started living in separate houses in August.

In October 2013, the divorce, the one I had been threatening since 1995, finally went through.

Wade and I were married for twenty-one years, together twenty-four. It wasn't all misery. We could have fun together, and Wade made me laugh, but I'm not sure there was ever true love there. It's actually quite impressive when you think about it that we lasted for decades given the terms of our engagement. Maybe I should have said no when he asked, or at least the following morning when I could comprehend what yes would mean. But then I wouldn't have my children. And I wouldn't have proven to myself what I could do. I don't hate Wade, but I would have if I stayed. And more importantly, I would have hated myself.

Our three-story rental house in Waxhaw,
North Carolina, where we hosted our
neighborhood Thanksgivings.

2004. Mom and Dad at a family event.

9
THE REST OF THE FAMILY, 1992–2021

*One of the biggest lies ever told is, "Blood makes you family." No blood
makes you related; loyalty, love, and trust makes you family.*

—PRINCE EA

While Wade and I were starting a family and making our way, albeit clumsily, through married life, the rest of my family was doing the same. We continued to get together periodically for holidays and family gatherings as long as Wade and I lived in Michigan, but my family wasn't really all that close. Each of us moved on to create separate lives, as siblings and parents do, with predictable touchpoints but almost no crossover.

Standing up to Don at age nineteen was a watershed moment, a separation between being my brothers' victim and becoming a person who could and did say "No!" While our collective childhoods were so insidiously intertwined, our lives as we matured really couldn't have been more different.

As an adult, David was a dick.

I hate saying that because his children will read this, but it's true. He always thought he was Mr. Cool, but in reality he was just a drunk pothead who could get a job but never keep it.

After high school, he worked a couple of odd jobs, including at a factory, but he would always either quit or get fired because he'd show up late or high or drunk or both. Eventually, my mom hired him on as a second manager at her Christian bookstore. We all thought this was a crazy idea, but he needed a job, and she hoped that if he worked for her, he might be more respectful.

She was wrong.

Every day, David was responsible for taking the money from the store cash register to the bank for deposit. Whoever thought this was the right responsibility to give a man with serious addiction issues was out of their own mind. Apparently, David started depositing only the checks, keeping whatever cash was in the bank envelope for himself. Eventually, his theft was discovered, but not before he had pocketed around $10,000 from my mom's store.

I remember the yelling, not at David, necessarily, but between Mom and Dad as they argued about what to do. I silently begged my parents to have him arrested, to press charges, if not to hold him responsible, at least to potentially force him to get the help he needed. But we were never a family that confronted our demons; instead, they covered it up, like I knew they would. I was incredulous, the anger threatening to finally make me say out loud the thoughts that were screaming through my mind: *Your son stole from his own mother and you're still going to put up with his bullshit?* If ever there was validation for why I didn't tell them about the abuse as a child, it was this. They would have swept it under the rug, our family's reputation more important than justice.

David got his first wife pregnant when he was twenty. They went on to have two more kids together. Eventually, she left him for another man who owned a business in Kansas. She moved herself and the kids there hoping for a better life. David saw them maybe once a year thereafter. He never had any money to help out with them and certainly wasn't in a position to be a stable father figure. He got married twice more . . . and divorced twice more.

I wish I could offer more, some redemption story or change of heart, but there isn't one. His life has quite literally been one set of bad decisions after another.

Despite what he did to me, it was hard to witness. Mom always said David was the smartest of all of us, had the most potential. He was born into a family where literally everything was given to him. Why couldn't he turn that into a life he could be proud of? I never understood why he threw everything away, why the drugs and the booze were more important than his job, his wife, or his kids. I guess addiction robs the good from almost any situation, but I have to wonder if there was more to it than that. Why did he start drinking and smoking pot so early? And why didn't he ever try to stop?

* * *

David claims he never knew about Don's sexual assaults. It seems odd to me that both brothers could abuse the same sister without some sort of familial awareness, but my parents never found out, so I guess it's possible David didn't know about Don, and Don didn't know about David either.

When I stood up to Don that last time, some demarcation line was drawn in the sands of time between our childhood and adulthood. Don never approached me again after that, and, from what I could tell, he actually became a good man. It's difficult to explain how I can say that given what he did to me, but that line is the separation between a stupid hormonal teenager who hurt his sister and a grown man who has become a decent person. Somehow, since that day, I have always known the difference.

At nineteen, Don got a job at Acheson Colloids Company, the biggest factory in town. He ended up putting himself through school while working full time. Don wanted to go to chiropractor college, but our dad lost his job at about the same time, and my parents didn't have the money to help Don with that goal. They told him chiropractic school was too expensive and suggested he attend the local community college for a few years. This became a bone of contention when my parents later paid for Dale and me to go to college. Don made it known that he thought I was a spoiled brat, one of his many jabs over the years.

Don did end up marrying the woman he was seeing when he was twenty-four and adopted her baby girl as his own. The two of them went on to have another daughter together before ultimately getting divorced. I'm not entirely sure why or who divorced whom. About a decade later, Don met and married his current wife Dee, who has two boys of her own. Like any blended family, they had their challenges, especially as the girls were growing up, but they seemed to do their best to create a stable environment for everyone. At least, that's as much as I could tell as we only saw them for holidays and special events like birthdays or the annual Memorial Day and Labor Day parties at Mom and Dad's. Once we moved down to Charlotte, our visits became even more infrequent, contained to the two weeks each summer we spent in Michigan, splitting time between my family and Wade's.

In 2009, the company Don worked for announced that they would be closing the factory in Port Huron by 2011. They gave some of their management team, like Don, the opportunity to take positions at their other locations. Ironically, there was a job opening at a plant in Charlotte. Knowing Don was considering it, Mom surprised me by asking if he could live with me for three to six months while he and Dee looked for a house and prepared to move. I was told he would almost never be there as he would be working all week and planned to house hunt or go back to Michigan on the weekends.

At the time, we lived in a huge 5,000 square foot house with a finished basement we rarely used. I couldn't say no. While I was somewhat hesitant, what reason could I possibly give my mom for why we couldn't help Don out in this way?

Sierra was thirteen at the time, and I remember thinking, *Should I be worried about this?* And maybe I should have been, but honestly, I knew this was the adult Don, the father Don, the man Don, not the teenage Don. Wade and I talked about it and decided that Don was not to be alone in the house with the kids, so if one of us was traveling, the other would not. Also, the door coming up from the basement, where he stayed, was right outside our master bedroom. We left our master bedroom door open when we slept so we could easily hear the kids in the middle of the night. There was no way Don would be able to get upstairs to the kids' rooms without one of us waking up. These things tamped down the mild anxiety I had about the situation, but in reality, none of the precautions really ended up being necessary. Our place wasn't a temporary home for Don; it was more like a way station. He did come home from work late and was gone most weekends, and we were too busy with our own work and the kids' activities to accommodate his schedule. My mom ended up being right; we rarely saw Don. To this day Sierra doesn't remember him living with us at all, even though he technically did for almost six months.

I guess it goes to show you that people can change, and that the mistakes of our past don't have to follow us into our future.

Or do they?

*   *   *

I never did tell Mom and Dad about what happened to me.

After I left for Michigan State, they decided there was no need for them to continue to maintain the blue saltbox house in Port Huron. It was way too big for just the two of them, and after raising five kids, the idea of downsizing seemed nice. So, they sold the house about the same time I moved out to attend MSU. It was a mixed blessing for me. I loved that house. There were so many good memories there, but it was also the keeper of my secret, so there was some relief when they sold it. I needed to move my life forward, but I needed the finality of never having to go back to that house to help me along.

My parents bought a small condo in Marysville, Michigan, just south of Port Huron. What a huge mistake! They hated living there. The place was way too small to host family gatherings or holidays and what they gained in lack of maintenance they lost in functionality.

My dad ended up getting a job just outside of Brooklyn, Michigan, about a two-hour drive from Marysville. Mom still had the Christian bookstore in Port Huron, so she stayed in the Marysville-Port Huron area and Dad commuted back and forth. At first, he lived in an apartment while they looked for a lot to purchase on Lake Columbia in Brooklyn. The process of building a custom home took awhile, but once it was completed, it was exactly what they wanted—big enough to host family gatherings but manageable for where they were in life. At the time, the bookstore was doing quite well financially, so the hope was to keep it going for a while to help fund their retirement. After my father's heart attack, however, they decided it was too much to keep going back and forth and sold the bookstore to a big box store that moved into the new mall going up in Port Huron.

While it became their full-time home, the lake house was also an idyllic place for our families to gather for the holidays. We went there to celebrate the official start of summer for Memorial Day and then closed out the season with our annual Labor Day bash. My parents had a motor boat and a pontoon boat. All of us would water ski off the back of the boat and spend evenings tooling around the lake on the pontoon. Despite the fact that we were not emotionally close as a family, my parents wanted their kids and their grandchildren to have a place to come back to, a place to gather. That was their way of showing love.

My parents' relationship improved immensely once they became empty nesters. Looking back, I imagine it was quite stressful to have five kids, and I expect it took a toll on their relationship, especially when we were young. My parents lived out very traditional gender roles and that bled over into the way they treated each other as well.

My dad could be condescending to my mom and clearly believed that her job was the house and the kids and his job was to work. She often complained about his drinking. While never an alcoholic, Dad would come home from work and drink four-to-six beers a night or, riling her up even more, he would go straight from work to the bar. She complained about it constantly, and I couldn't understand why she wouldn't just leave if she was so miserable. One night, I watched from my bedroom window as Mom sat in her car in the driveway after one of their fights. My dad, bent at the waist, elbows on the driver's side windowsill, leaning in to try and talk her into staying. I whispered, "Just go already. If you hate it here so much, just leave." That was more typical of our household. We didn't talk openly about anything; we just whispered from windows what was going on behind the panes.

Of course, to be fair, I didn't understand marriage back then nor the way women trap themselves in a commitment loop they can't get out of. I see now the similarities in my parents' marriage and my own marriage with Wade. While I played a different role than my mother, the frustration, the loneliness, the complaining all feels acutely familiar.

*   *   *

I think all of us kids finally leaving is what saved them. Ultimately, their marriage was based on a foundation of love and companionship, which they rediscovered in the years after we left home.

That, and, my dad's dementia. When Dad was in his late seventies, we started noticing that he had become forgetful. Assuming it was normal aging, we didn't think much of it, until he started repeating the same questions over and over again. We finally suggested to

Mom that he get checked out. Dad was diagnosed with a slow, but progressive form of dementia. Medication helped, but as Dad aged into his eighties, the forgetfulness started getting more serious. Mom was smart enough to tie a red ribbon to the antenna of his car, partly so he could find it in a big parking lot, and partly so she could find *him* if he went missing. That turned out to be a stroke of brilliance when one day Dad walked out the front door without so much as a peep about where he was going and never came back. Mom found him sitting in the driver's seat of his van in the local IGA grocery-store parking lot, red ribbon flapping in the wind.

As the dementia got worse, my dad became more dependent on my mom, and it was as if the entirety of his tough exterior melted. He was a giant teddy bear around her, grateful for her mere presence and certainly for her assistance in a way he never had been when we were growing up.

Once the lake house got to be too much for them to keep up with, Mom and Dad moved into a cute ranch house on a golf course. It worked well for them for a number of years, but the house still had a set of stairs that led to the basement where all of dad's prized possessions were stored. The trip up and down those stairs became increasingly more dangerous as his cognition failed. Additionally, Dad had a limp leg, the long-term side effect of transferring the vein in his leg to his heart during his open heart surgery years before. It was only a matter of time before he fell, so all of us kids decided we had to get our parents out of the "death trap."

What followed was a literal nightmare that I largely brought on myself because instead of prioritizing just getting them in a safe, affordable place, I wanted them to have some agency over where they lived. Dale was the only child left in Michigan by that point, so it made more sense to move Mom and Dad down to North Carolina where both Don and I lived. My mom was adamant that they would not consider a senior-living facility, but we convinced them that Dad needed some additional help and being around people their own age might help them build community. That was an epic fail. The place was only fifteen minutes from Don and right on the lake in Davidson, North Carolina. Despite having a corner unit with a beautiful view, Mom cried every day. "I'm the only healthy person here," she would wail. The facility was shocked when we moved them out as no one had ever left the place of their own accord before.

Two more failed attempts left all of us exhausted. Each time Mom said no, I would go back to the drawing board, consulting my spreadsheet of options and starting over with the phone calls. She didn't want to live in an "old folks home," and she thought renting was "throwing away money"—we just couldn't win. She wanted to be in her own home, and if that was no longer possible, then she wanted to buy a new one so, at ninety years old, my parents bought a new construction, two-bedroom, two-bath house in a fifty-five and over community right near where I was getting ready to move.

I just wanted her to make a decision she could stick with. I couldn't empathize with her loss of independence at the time because I was so blinded by the work of trying to find them a place to live. In my mind, these places were good enough, but I might have known that my mother was intent on keeping her upper-middle-class dignity. She didn't want to be told she was old, and she certainly didn't want her daughter telling her where to live.

Unsurprisingly, this living situation soon became problematic as my dad certainly shouldn't have been driving, and it was becoming difficult for my mom as well. Dad was still fairly indignant about driving, not understanding that his dementia made him a serious liability on the road. We learned that if we gave Dad the keys to hold, we could convince him that Mom or their helper should be the one to drive. Something about the way his brain was now functioning could make peace with that compromise.

I hired a cleaning crew to come tidy Mom and Dad's house every other week. I was working from home one day when I got a frantic call from the cleaning lady. She said that Mom was in extreme pain and that they had called 911. I ran out the door and arrived just as the ambulance was pulling up. The EMTs wanted to take her to the emergency room because the EKG showed signs of cardiac distress. As I climbed into my car to follow the ambulance, I looked out to see my dad, seated in his chair, staring out the window at the ambulance. He couldn't understand what was happening but knew something was wrong with Mom. I ran back in to check on him. The cleaning ladies had tears in their eyes as I gave him a big hug and gently explained that Mom needed to go to the hospital. One of their neighbors kindly volunteered to sit with him, but it broke my heart to leave him like that.

I have never felt more helpless than I did that day. Not only because I couldn't take care of my dad and my mom at the same time, but because at the hospital, Mom screamed nonstop for hours. She was in agonizing pain and just kept begging someone, anyone, to help her. The emergency room team was moving as fast as they could to find out what was wrong with her so they could treat her appropriately, but knowing that doesn't take the pain away. I will never be able to unhear the sound of my mom's animal-like keening.

The emergency room team finally came to the conclusion that she had had a heart attack and that part of her heart was dead. She was rushed to the intensive care unit but rapidly deteriorated. Dale and his family hit the road immediately, hoping to make it in time to be with her, but not David. He couldn't be bothered. When I called to tell him, his response was, "I have a cat. I have to take care of my cat. Do you want me to come while she's dying or do you want me to come to the funeral because I can't come to both?" Even when we all volunteered to pay for his flight, he resisted. I wasn't shocked at his reaction, just perpetually disappointed.

It became clear fairly quickly that Mom was going to die. Her care team recommended removing all life support, which we agreed to once it was explained that there was nothing they could do for her other than to keep her comfortable. This was February 2021 and COVID protocols were still in place, meaning only two visitors and only those that were immediate family were allowed in to see Mom. We removed all of the machines at 5:30 p.m. on February 12, having been assured that she would go quickly. I convinced the hospital to allow myself, Dad, Dale, and Don into the room at the same time to say our goodbyes. Unexpectedly, though, Mom made it through the night, and the hospital staff finally kicked us out around midnight. The following morning, I had to have another negotiation with the hospital to try and get Becky, Dale's wife, and their son Zach, in to see Mom. They told me we had met our quota the night before. I was furious! Mom was a person, not a quota!

Undeterred, I persisted, my desperation that she not be alone at the end overcoming any hesitancy at pushing the hospital's boundaries. It took forever to get the approval, so I told Dale and his family to go take showers and not to rush. They were still in their hotel room when we got the call. Mom was gone.

As much as I know it's not my fault, I feel guilty to this day that I told them to take their time, that I played some part in them not getting to say goodbye. I'm the one that never wanted to be alone, so it is agonizing for me to think of her in her final moments without at least one of us there. But maybe that's more about me than it is about her. When I hear her voice in my head, its intonation is not sadness that she died alone but the martyrdom she constantly carried with her in life. Ever the victim, I can hear the lonely disbelief . . . "They're not coming back. They knew I was still alive, but I guess they let me go." It never would have occurred to her that we were fighting to get back to her and just missed our chance.

For weeks after Mom died, I was tormented by feeling like I should have been a better daughter, should have been kinder to her, should have tried harder to have a deeper relationship with her. It's one of the reasons I took on so much responsibility to help my dad after her death.

I didn't want to live with the same guilt twice.

*   *   *

Unbeknownst to me at the time, moving Mom and Dad down to North Carolina became the catalyst that ignited a volcanic eruption. Seeing as how Don was less than an hour's drive from Mom and Dad when they moved to the house near me, it made sense that we would share some of the responsibilities of caring for them and that he would consistently come visit them. At first, we agreed that we would alternate weekends to visit. I didn't really want to be there when he was there, and I was trying to maintain a life of my own as well. That plan worked well for a while, but then he started going every three weeks or just once a month or would call me on a Friday night to say he was going to visit the next day on one of my weekends. This infuriated me. Not only was there zero respect for me or my time, I now felt like I was responsible for making sure my parents weren't alone. My anger at Don became like lava, heating up inside me, the pressure building. An eruption was inevitable. I just had no idea what all it would unleash.

Part III

Shattering the Silence

2012. Me and Tom on our first vacation together in Marco Island, Florida.

10
The Volcano, May 2021

The most dangerous anger comes from someone with a good heart.
They hold it in, they stay calm, they forgive until one day they
can't anymore . . . Don't push a good person too far.
—ROBIN WILLIAMS

I married Tom one month after my divorce with Wade was final. That sounds like some sordid affair, but it was really just the antiquated rules of the North Carolina divorce laws.

When I officially filed for divorce from Wade in March 2012, I told him I was going to start dating other people. At the time, Match.com was all the rage, so I built a profile. I didn't spend much time on my own description. I uploaded old, grainy pictures figuring my handle—"laughs-lots-is-good"—was sufficient in describing the kind of person I was. I was far more focused on selecting the criteria for my future mate. My list of must haves was meticulously honed, based, unsurprisingly, on all of the things Wade wasn't. I had settled once, and there was no way I was going to do that again. Given that I almost missed out on meeting Tom altogether, I may have gone a bit overboard with what I would and wouldn't accept in a match, but I just didn't want to waste my time with another guy who couldn't be my equal. I finally knew what I wanted in a man, and I wasn't going to settle for any less.

Despite my lackadaisical effort at building my own profile, I attracted quite a few suitors. As anyone who's been on a dating site has probably experienced, it can feel like a full-time job to wade through everyone who makes contact. Three Mikes, two Steves. This one had two kids, that one was an architect. This one was allergic to shellfish, that one loved sushi. I just couldn't keep it all straight. Ever the pragmatist, I developed an epic spreadsheet with all of my matches' characteristics. If one of them called me, I'd bolt for my computer to pull up my sheet before I got too deep into the conversation, terrified I'd mix up one Steve with another Mike. It was ridiculous. My friends joked that I should have patented that spreadsheet and sold it for good money once I found Tom. They were probably right.

It's no surprise that by that September, six months later, I was over it. I decided one night that I was going to suspend my subscription, but I wanted to take one more look before I officially gave up. On Match, in addition to seeing who has "winked" at you, you can also see who has viewed your profile but passed you by. I started going through those profiles and stopped on one in particular. I saw that this guy hadn't made it to my matches because his associate's degree didn't align with my high-bar criteria. He was super cute, and his profile was hilarious. It was obvious he had seen my profile and said nothing! I was pissed! What was wrong with me that this guy didn't want to at least wink at me? Fueled by my righteous indignation, I sent him a coy message—"Hey, I think you winked at me so just wanted to say hello"—knowing full well he absolutely had not.

The next morning, a message from Tom was in my inbox. He did think I was attractive, and he had been interested, but because his experience on Match had been of women whose photos looked nothing like their actual appearance, he was worried that he couldn't actually tell what I looked like from my grainy photos. His response to my message, "Nah . . . Winking is for sissies," made me laugh. We started emailing back and forth and the communication took off from there.

I was traveling for work a ton at the time, and so was he, so it took a few months for our schedules to align so we could go on a date. In the interim, we just talked. For hours. I got to know him extremely well, so by the time we met in person, I was already pretty taken with this guy. We totally hit it off on our first date, and it didn't take Tom long to lay down the gauntlet. "You want to be with me? You only get me. If you want to date other people, I'm going to walk away." At first, I was a little put out. Who did he think he was? But I was also a little impressed.

I needed a Viking. Tom was my Viking.

*   *   *

We got engaged in July 2013.

Wade and I had officially been separated, i.e. living in differ-ent houses, for a year at that point, part of those antiquated North

Carolina laws, and the final divorce papers were imminent. Tom had built a solid relationship with my kids, and he was planning to move into the house that I was renting so the kids wouldn't have to change schools. We had briefly talked about what we wanted for our wedding, but I wasn't in my twenties this time, so the wedding itself took a backseat to us being together.

That fall, Tom was between jobs for a period of time, but as a type I diabetic, he really couldn't take the risk of being without health insurance. I knew if we got married, I could cover him under my health insurance. So, while vacationing with good friends in California that November, I got the inspiration that we should elope. We would still plan a ceremony with our friends and family at some point in the future, but the most imminent issue was ensuring Tom had coverage. It may not have been the way we envisioned starting our life together, but it was small and special, and we are both practical people, so it made sense at the time. The only problem is we didn't tell the kids.

Unfortunately, Sierra, my eldest, found out. She was going through photos on my computer and found a folder titled "Tom and Darlene wedding." Understandably, she was incredibly upset, and what seemed like a reasonable decision at the time turned into something much more egregious. At that point, we told her brothers and everyone else. Our intentions in keeping the wedding from them were good, even if the execution went sideways. We were trying to protect them from any more pain after all they had been through with the divorce. But, I should have known that secrets carry their own hurt.

We did ultimately hold a beautiful wedding ceremony in St. Kitts a year and a half later with our closest friends, Tom's brother and his wife, and the kids in attendance. While we had technically been married for a while at that point, this was an opportunity for us to make a public commitment in front of those dearest to us.

Tom was such a positive influence for the kids. Never having had any of his own, he was the perfect stepfather . . . when I let him. When we got married, Sierra was sixteen and the twins just twelve, and I was incredibly protective of them. I got defensive any time Tom stepped in to try and be the disciplinarian, as if his actions were insinuating that I was a bad mom and couldn't manage them on my own. It created serious discord between the two of us.

That wasn't our only struggle. My personal mantra of always having to win, born from an intense determination to never let David or Don see me fail, meant that I always had to be right. To me, winning *was* surviving. What I didn't realize is that this tactic that worked to help me survive my childhood abuse wreaked havoc on my other relationships. Tom would often complain that I just wouldn't give an inch. If there was a disagreement, I was willing to fight it out until he acquiesced to my point of view. Oftentimes, he would just walk away, muttering "You're impossible." In those moments, a defensive litany would roll on repeat through my head, "I don't need this. I don't need anyone. I did this alone as a kid. I can do it alone now."

It took years of therapy to understand that if you always have to win, it means you are always in a battle, and the other person isn't your husband. He's your opponent.

*   *   *

Tom and I had our own issues, yes, but he was the complete opposite of Wade when it came to supporting me and our family. He was a fierce protector, so much so that any time Don was invited to our house, it started a fight between Tom and me. I had told him about the abuse before we were married. I actually kind of blindsided him when we were out to dinner one night. We were talking about our commitment to each other, how we were falling in love and wanted a future together. That old litany of "I don't deserve this kind of love" clicked on in my head. I started crying over my bento box and the tears just wouldn't stop. People at the surrounding tables began to stare. I was embarrassed and Tom was concerned, having no idea why I was so upset. By the time I got out what had caused all that emotion, he was so relieved I wasn't leaving him that it took a while for what I told him to sink in.

And then he was livid.

Tom wanted retribution. A Brooklyn native, Tom was wired to handle this man to man, a confrontation where he could demand, in his words, "a fucking apology." If I wasn't going to fight for little Darlene, Tom was ready to. But I wouldn't let him. I knew that if that confrontation got physical or out of control in any way, Mom and Dad would find out, and I couldn't have that. I had protected them from the truth for forty years; what good would come from them finding out now?

But Tom's reaction spurred something in me. Maybe I did deserve an apology. In all this time, I had never once considered confronting my brothers, but with Tom by my side, I started to think it was a conversation I could have. All I wanted was an apology, after all. No one else had to know.

For weeks, I worked up the courage to call Don. Every time I thought about doing it, I would shake violently, but the idea had taken hold, and I'm not one to abandon an idea once I've committed to it. With Tom on the bed whispering messages of support, I cocooned myself in our closet, about the only place in a house with three kids and three dogs that I could find privacy. I dialed.

"Hey. There's something that's really been bothering me and I'd like to have a conversation," I said, hand sweating as I held the phone to my ear.

"Sure," Don replied.

"I really need your help. I need to get through what you did to me, and the way to get through what you did to me is to just please say you're sorry because I don't want to live in this box. I don't want this burden anymore."

Silence.

And then the words I'll never forget. "Oh really. I didn't think it bothered you that bad."

Shock descended over my system. I'm not even sure what was said after that, but I hung up the phone and just sat there, surrounded by dresses and shoes and the symbols of a normal life. How could he have said that? With such nonchalance, like I might have even enjoyed being raped. I'll never understand it. Was it really too much to just apologize?

*   *   *

After that, trying to convince Tom to hold the dogs at bay, so to speak, was increasingly challenging. Until my parents moved to North Carolina, we really only saw Don on holidays or at significant family events, but Tom and I would inevitably get in a fight days before their arrival. We did our best to keep it together, but it was incredibly difficult to swallow that kind of hurt and put on a happy face. I had decades of practice at this, of course, but it was new for Tom.

"It's wrong on so many levels!" he would say, angry that he had to voluntarily let this man who had raped his wife into his house. And not just let him in, but be nice to him, welcoming, pretend that they were all family. It was asking a lot, and I knew it.

Things changed when Don and I started having to work together to care for Mom and Dad, especially after Mom died.

When Mom passed away, we knew Dad couldn't stay in the house alone. He even told us he didn't want to. But finding the right place for him was difficult. I wanted him near me, but Don didn't think it was fair that he had to drive double the distance that I did to see Dad. I gave in, trying to keep the peace but already knowing I was going to be the one to do the majority of the caretaking.

We found an assisted living facility as close to halfway between Don and me as possible. It was about an hour drive for me, and about forty minutes for Don. It was a beautiful facility, and at over $7,000 per month, it should be. It took about six weeks to get Dad a room there. In the interim, he lived with Tom and me in my son's old bedroom. I wanted to do this for my dad, to care for him, so that he would not be alone, especially as his dementia-addled brain struggled to grasp all of the changes coming at him so quickly. But, it was hard.

Dad wet the bed. And my couch. I wasn't prepared for that. For my own father's incontinence. For having to convince him to wear diapers to bed. For the embarrassment I felt for both of us at having to ask. We had never shared that kind of intimacy or interdependence when I was growing up, and it was awkward for both of us to establish it out of necessity as adults.

When we finally moved Dad into his new room, we did so with some measure of relief. Beyond just having him in a place that was better equipped to care for him, I also thought Don and I would now be able to go back to splitting duties, somewhat like we'd tried to do when Mom was still alive. We set up a calendar, agreeing to alternate weekends to visit Dad. That worked . . . until it didn't. As time went on, Don's visits became more erratic. He'd call me on Friday night to tell me he was going to skip his weekend and come the next, my weekend. Or, I'd go visit Dad and realize he hadn't been shaved or his nails hadn't been trimmed. Little things, but things *I* was doing to care for Dad, so I couldn't understand why Don couldn't do them too. The frustration mounted. And then Dad's phone stopped working. Such a simple thing to fix. Instead, it was what broke everything apart.

* * *

Dad was now alone, and while he lived in a beautiful place with caring staff, his only connection to us, his children, was his phone. I couldn't stand the idea of him being unable to reach us whenever he wanted. He complained that the phone wasn't working, so I tested it myself when I went to visit and confirmed that there was no dial tone. In advance of Don's visit the following weekend, I called the phone company who assured me that it was not the phone itself but the building that had been out of service and that it should be working now. I told Don as much and asked him to test the phone when he arrived.

When I knew he was at Dad's, I shot him a quick text: *Were u able to get the phone fixed?*

He answered no, regurgitating the story about the building phone lines being down. At that point, I tried calling him to clarify what was going on but he wouldn't pick up. I called a second time after more pointless texts but again, he didn't pick up. At that point, I lost my temper.

(Me) *U r being a total ass.*

(Me) *If you actually returned peoples phone calls when they called you we wouldn't be in this text messaging situation.*

(Don) *You do not listen! You do not read!*

(Me) *OMG. Just stop. And you don't ever return anybody's phone calls. Stop being a total child*

(Don) *I'm not! Listen to yourself!*

(Me) *I am not going to listen to your stupidity.*

(Me) *You are right. I refuse to listen to that*

(Don) *Please!*

(Don) *All this is because you cannot read*

(Me) *I'd be very very careful how you talk to me and treat me as I could completely destroy your life if you want me to*

(Me) *Since you completely destroyed my entire childhood and upbringing. Rapist.*

(Don) *Wow! Go for it! Right now!*

The volcano inside of me erupted. The fifty years of secrets, shame, and shattered innocence overflowing. The lack of an apology, the years of having to pretend like everything was fine. Mom was dead. Dad's dementia made him incapable of holding on to the current moment, much less the past. There was nothing holding me back anymore. My fingers flew over the phone, my rage palpable, as I text-shouted at the Don of our childhood, the Don that raped me, the one who told me to be quiet, who threatened me, who hunted me.

I was no longer communicating with my adult brother. I was letting loose on my rapist.

Eventually, I ran out of steam, and knowing that we had friends coming over, I stopped texting, not wanting to deal with this while our company was there.

During dinner that night, Dad called me. When I saw "Dad" pop up on my phone screen, I immediately excused myself and stepped out to take the call. I have no idea how he used the phone in his own room seeing as how it supposedly wasn't working earlier that day, but it didn't matter at that point. He was distressed, worried about his sisters, and asked me to move money into their accounts immediately. Given that both of his sisters had died five and seven years prior, it was clear that he was really out of sorts. This type of thing was not uncommon as his dementia worsened. I had no idea what caused this agitation, but I needed Don to help me settle him down. So I texted again . . .

(Me) *Let's put the swords down.*

(Me) *Dad just called saying he wants to talk to Aunt Corine and Arlene about their finances and wants me to move money from his account to his sisters.*

(Don) *I don't know what you are thinking!*

(Me) *What r u talking about? Seriously!*

(Don) *If you think something happened, I am absolutely sorry! There was never anything that would have constituted rape!*

(Me) *Y don't u & I talk this thru 1:1 someday. I'm sorry too.*

(Me) *Thanks for saying sorry.*

I meant that. It was all I had ever wanted. An apology. It sounds crazy, but I never had any intention of blowing up Don's life. I honestly never had any intention of telling anyone that didn't already know. I just wanted him to know that I hadn't forgotten, that he couldn't treat me like shit anymore and get away with it. I guess it could have been over there. Maybe it was my compulsive need to win, or just an itching desire to have the last word, but I wasn't quite ready to let it go yet. I tried calling him, but he wouldn't pick up.

(Me) *I hate you because you are such a liar.*

(Don) *Your a nutt bag!*

I thought the initial eruption was enough, that I had been purged of the pressure of the fire building inside me. But no, it was actually just smoldering, waiting for a second chance to explode. I know I should have put the phone down, but I didn't. And what came after isn't flattering to anyone.

(Me) *Fuck off you lie.*

(Me) *Don't you ever fucking come near me again and don't you dare go near my father again*

(Me) *You are such a fucking liar!!*

(Me) *I hope you burn in hell for this*

(Don) *You are out of control!*

The texts may have sounded out of control, but I wasn't. I was just channeling fifty years of rage. It didn't get better from there. The tirade continued. At some point, Don must have handed his phone over to his wife Dee, who asked me where Tom was. She suggested I had maybe had too much to drink and wanted Tom to call her. That infuriated me even more. Not only was she blind to the truth, but now she was insinuating that my anger was simply a byproduct of overindulging, not holding on to the secret of her husband raping me. I had no intention of involving Tom, knowing that he would see this as his opportunity to rip their heads off, escalating the situation even further. I kept going.

(Me) *Tell Don he needs to go find a fucking shrink to get over raping his little sister.*

Dee's texts started with a placating tone, as if she was talking to a child having a temper tantrum, but the more I pushed back, the more her tone sharpened to match mine. I obviously have no idea what back and forth might have been going on between her and Don on their end of the phone, but eventually, this text came through.

(Dee) *Ok then. I think you need help it never happened. We are getting a lawyer ad sewing you!*
(Me) *Go for it honey!!*

*   *   *

I got home from dinner at around 10 p.m., and my phone started blowing up.

Bailey, Don's daughter, sent me a message via Facebook. "Hi, I am not sure what is going on . . ."

I couldn't believe it. Don must have called his daughter as fast as he could, afraid that I might get to her first. Except, I never had any intention of calling her. Or anyone else, for that matter. This was between me and Don, and it could have stayed that way.

Kristen, Don's other daughter, was next. Her message suggested Don had called her and told her I was having a nervous breakdown and had gone crazy. "Can we talk tomorrow?" she requested.

At this point I was bawling. I was stunned. Hours before, my secret had been safely boxed up and now, everyone knew. Or, at least, they knew something, whatever Don had told them. I made plans to talk with Kristen the following morning and went to bed, trying to sleep through the nightmares. I woke knowing there was one person I had to talk to before anyone else. The only other person who also had a secret. David.

I grabbed my phone and texted him, asking if he was available to chat. He was.

I went into my office and closed the door. I took a deep breath, trying to calm my shaking body. Butterflies bounced around in my stomach as I picked up the phone and dialed David's number. I thought I was going to throw up, but I needed to know. Needed to be sure that I hadn't really gone crazy. I didn't say anything to David about the text volcano with Don, and it was clear that Don had not called him yet. Hesitantly, I said, "There's something that's been bugging me for a really long time. I just need to know. Did you abuse me when I was little? Like sexually assault me?"

David took a big breath, a sigh shuddering out from the other end of the line. "Yeah. I am a piece of shit. I made some really stupid decisions in my younger days." My shoulders dropped away from my ears. I hadn't even realized they had been there. Here it was. A simple acknowledgement of what happened. It was the validation I needed. David went on to apologize. He seemed almost incredulous himself, like he couldn't believe he had done that to me. The tears started to roll, but I could feel the butterflies settling, their flight interrupted by the truth finally making its way to my ears.

"Thank you," I said. I knew his apology was sincere. And that was all I wanted. I just needed to be acknowledged. To have what was done to me recognized as real.

David was the drunk. The drug addict. The loser who could never hold a job. The thief. I doubt anyone would have been that surprised if I accused him of assaulting me. And yet, he's the one who said "I'm sorry."

Don? Yeah. He's the one who ended up suing me.

2023, Charleston, South Carolina. Me and Sierra at the rooftop restaurant that fateful night.

11

RELIVING THE TRAUMA, 2021–2024

I sat with my anger long enough until she told me her real name was grief.

—C. S. LEWIS

Oh, shit, I thought, as tears ran down my face. The realization hit me all at once as I tried to respond to the messages from Don's daughters. "I'm going to have to tell my kids."

I was no longer in control. The secret was out of its box. For the past fifty years, I had guarded that box, a sentry protecting the secret and those who would be most hurt by it. My parents may have no longer needed protecting, but my children still did. Somehow, in confronting Don for my own sanity, I had failed at my duties. The secret was now free, and the consequences of that had only just begun to hit me.

I was devastated. How could I tell my babies what had happened to me? No child should have to hear that about their mother. Or their uncles, for that matter. I felt incredibly vulnerable and scared. What would they think of me once they knew?

We were scheduled to leave for a big family vacation to Zion National Park two weeks after the volcano erupted, and I was determined that Don was not going to ruin that trip for me and my family. The weekend after the initial text blow up, I gathered Austin and Jake, my boys, and sat them down. I can't even imagine what they thought was happening as I started crying before I even got one word out. I felt like I couldn't breathe, literally choking as I tried to force words out of my mouth.

I told them I was sexually assaulted by their uncles David and Don when I was a child.

I told them it had been a secret I kept for the past fifty years, but that the secret was now out and Don was telling our family members that I was a liar and had a nervous breakdown.

I told them that I didn't know what would happen now.

I told them how sorry I was that I failed to protect them from this pain.

I am incredibly proud of my sons. They are good men who have faced their own demons, but I swear I have never been prouder of them than in that moment when the shock started to fade from their faces and nothing but love and support followed. They didn't hate me. They weren't disgusted by me. And, my deepest fear relieved, they were not going to abandon me.

I told Sierra separately, not really intentionally, but more so out of needing to find a time when I could get her in person. Sierra had recently gone through an emotional break up and was in the process of moving to her own apartment that was forty-five minutes away from our house. I didn't want to tell her over the phone and knew she was coming home to stay for a few days before we left for vacation. She arrived in the middle of the work day, and came to find me in my office. It probably wasn't the best time to drop this in her lap, for her or me, but I wasn't sure when there would be another time. Sitting across from her, my desk between us, my heart broke as I watched her face slowly shift as she heard the details of my abuse. Like her brothers, she was stunned, but incredibly supportive. It's uncanny how perceptive a daughter can be with their own mother's pain. At one point, she said, "Mom, it sounds like you still haven't forgiven yourself and the only way to heal is to forgive yourself first." Those words stayed with me throughout everything that happened thereafter as I learned, painstakingly slowly, how to give myself grace.

*   *   *

Telling my kids about my childhood sexual abuse was hard enough, but knowing that Don was spreading lies about me to my entire family was too much. The story he concocted that I was having a nervous breakdown, that I was a drunk, and a liar, was untenable to me. I was mad, yes, but I was also unwilling to let that narrative stand. Knowing that the text messages reflected the anger and desperation of a hurt little girl, I wanted to set the record straight from the voice of a competent, calm adult. So, I wrote an email to all three of my brothers. The subject line read "The Facts."

The email channeled my work voice: the collected, self-assured, detail-oriented Darlene. I laid out point by point what had happened to me, why I kept it secret all these years, the people closest to me that I had told, and why a sincere apology from Don would have made all of this go away. The process of writing the email was cathartic. It helped me dial all of my anger, all the anxiety, the internal swirling of the past few weeks and channel it into something that felt productive. I'm not sure exactly what I expected in response or if I even cared. I wrote the letter for me as an act of healing, an opportunity to finally tell my family the truth of what had happened to me. I knew the relationship with Don and David was over, and I was going to have to make peace with that, but it could have stopped there.

Instead, Don's response was swift, resolute in my status as a "psychopathic liar," and ended with what Tom took as a direct threat to our family. In hindsight, I can't say that I was surprised. The second Don handed his phone over to Dee to read his text messages that night, he made a conscious decision to lie. And keep lying.

Tom had been waiting for this exact moment, the unequivocal opportunity to directly confront Don. I couldn't hold the dogs back anymore. Tom called Don and left a voicemail. His prolific use of the f-word would make a sailor proud. I'm sure it just added fuel to the fire, but it's what Tom needed to do to protect his family, and frankly, it felt pretty fucking nice to be protected for once.

After the email exchange and the ensuing voicemail, things went quiet, at least for a month or so. I naively hoped we might have reached a truce, or at least, a willingness to stay in our respective corners. But, that hope was obliterated when I received a cease and desist letter on July 1. It would have been one thing if the letter had just commanded me to stop talking about the sexual abuse accusations. I hadn't been the one to share those with the family in the first place. But it was the demand for a signed, notarized statement fully recanting those accusations and asserting that Don is of "good moral character" that got me. There was no way in hell I was doing that.

The letter also declared that if a statement was not received, Don would "obtain relief permitted by the fullest extent allowed by the law." Ominous words. That afternoon, I posted in our neighborhood Facebook group asking for a recommendation for an attorney. Writing this, I realize how ridiculous it is that I searched for the attorney that would ultimately represent me in a defamation lawsuit through Facebook, but I was that unprepared for how far this situation had devolved. No matter how ridiculous it might have been, it worked, and I was referred to Jeffrey Kuykendal, whom I came to know as Jeff. From our first conversation, I knew I wanted him to represent me. He was competent, sincere, and direct. He advised me to completely ignore the cease and desist letters, even after I received a second one with a new due date for my statement. To his thinking, what was the point in responding if I had no intention of complying? Don had walked right up to my line in the sand, and I was ready to defend it if necessary.

*　　*　　*

Don filed his lawsuit against me on January 6, 2022. He was seeking a half million dollars in damages.

I know he and Dee had threatened to "sew" me. I just never believed he'd actually do it.

He claimed that because of me and my lies, he was no longer allowed to see his daughters or granddaughters. The irony is that I was the one who tried to convince both of his daughters *not* to shut him out of their lives. Despite what they had been told about me, our lines of communication remained open.

Jeff and I talked about our strategy. I had no desire to go to court, but I was adamant that I would not recant what I said because it was the absolute truth. Jeff believed me.

"What about countersuing him?" Jeff asked. I had honestly never thought about it; I was just concerned with defending myself. Jeff was prepared to build a strong defense, and while defense wins championships, he advised that even if we won, I would likely be out thousands of dollars in legal fees. Why not throw some offense in there in case there was a chance I could be awarded damages, particularly given the fact that Don's widespread claims of me being a psychopathic liar had absolutely caused me harm.

I sat with that. I didn't want to be here at all. I never wanted to sue Don. I wanted an apology. I got a lawsuit instead. But, why shouldn't I be entitled to damages too? The truth was on my side. I didn't need Don's money, nor did I want it. But I was incensed that the indignant asshole sued me over *his* lies, and now it was his turn to pay for his actions. I needed to take a stand, to fight for little Darlene, to be her voice.

We countersued, and what had been one trial, now became two. Don's lawsuit against me and my countersuit against him.

*   *   *

I learned more than I ever wanted to know about our judicial system, at least on the civil side, going through this process. As part of evidentiary discovery, Don and I had to be deposed. I've never been deposed before, but I made sure I was ready. I was determined not to be intimidated by Don or his attorneys. But boy did he try. I had given permission for Don to be there during the deposition but regretted it almost immediately as the hostility rolled off of him. I was seated at the head of the conference room table with Jeff and Tom to my left. Don sat farther down with his attorneys on the other side of the table and a videographer set up in the back of the room.

While I knew he would be physically present, I had no idea Don would take the extra step of paying close to $2,500 to videotape me, which was totally optional. Several times during my testimony, he would pound his pen on his notepad and vehemently scribble something he'd shoot across the table to his attorneys. When I went to speak, Don would lean in, trying to stare me down, shaking his head and mouthing "liar" in my direction. It got so bad that Tom noticed and started mimicking his movements to block Don from my line of sight. Don's head went forward and Tom's shot out in front of it. It would have been comical if it wasn't so ridiculous. It didn't matter though. I never wavered.

In contrast, Jeff and I felt like Don's deposition was rather weak. He actively evaded Jeff's questions, talked in circles, and even admitted he didn't know the definition of defamation in the state of North Carolina, the very thing he was suing me for.

In January 2023, we had to go through court-ordered mediation in a last ditch effort to settle this whole thing out of court. After the depositions, Jeff and I thought we were finally going to get somewhere as it was so clear that I would present as a credible witness on the stand. We had also created a case with substantial supporting documentation and witnesses that all spoke to a consistent account that I had been assaulted. From what we could tell, Don had nothing other than his indignation.

We suspect that Don's attorneys encouraged him to settle, but he refused. By the time we got to mediation, I had spent close to $30,000 on legal fees. I was willing to settle for $15,000 and be done with it and said as much to the mediator. The mediator was baffled. I guess it was rare to have a defendant demand that the *plaintiff* pay them a settlement, but I was feeling confident that if we went to trial, there was a strong chance I would win, so I saw no reason to fold. The mediator warned me to think long and hard about how ashamed and embarrassed I would be if I had to take the stand. I have no way of knowing, but I seriously doubt they teach the "shame and embarrassment" tactic at mediator school. Needless to say, I doubled down on my offer.

The mediator tried to get Don to make a counteroffer, and he did, for one dollar. Tom and I looked at each other. I could feel Tom's anger bubbling up, but I felt resolute. I looked back at the mediator, calm, and composed.

"I had time to think long and hard about what you said. And you know what? I've decided I won't be embarrassed. I won't be ashamed. In fact, it will feel incredible for a jury of my peers to hear me and *believe me.* So, no. I do not accept Don's disgusting offer. It's time for him to face the consequences of his actions." Tom took my hand, and we stood up and walked out.

While I was no longer afraid of taking the stand, by the end of January, I was bleeding money on legal fees and wanted to end this. I was also worried about Dad. The cost of his assisted living facility skyrocketed over the prior three years to more than $10,000 per month, and he was running out of money. I sent an email to Jeff with a final offer. Don didn't have to pay me a dime. If he put fifty thousand dollars into Dad's checking account to help pay for his care, this would be over. Jeff was shocked but agreed it was a fair and reasonable offer.

Don refused.

I was done. We were going to court.

*   *   *

After receiving the cease and desist letters back in July 2021, my nightmares returned with a vengeance. I have always had nightmares, at least ever since the abuse started, but prior to the volcano eruption, I had finally gotten them under control after years of therapy. They say the body keeps the score, with a memory for trauma that surpasses anything our conscious mind can control. I can only assume that being catapulted into this conflict with Don reignited that old trauma.

One night a few weeks after the first letter arrived, Tom woke up at two or three o'clock in the morning to find me beating on his chest, crying hysterically, and clearly fighting a demon he could not see. Poor Tom, before he could do anything, he had to remove his CPAP machine from around his head and get his breathing tape off his mouth. Once he was untethered and somewhat more awake, he finally understood that I was dreaming and gently but persistently forced me to wake up. When I finally came to, he asked, "What the hell happened?" Shaking violently, I cried, "Oh my God! You took everything from me. You took the house, the kids, the dogs, my job. I had nothing. I was alone." Rubbing my shoulder in true Tom fashion, he looked at me cockeyed and threw back, "Whoa, whoa, whoa, you know this has to be a nightmare because I'd never take your kids." His witty comeback made me laugh, and I could feel myself come down from the adrenaline of being attacked. I don't remember much of the dream, but that's what it felt like, like I and everything that mattered to me was under attack, and I was fighting for my life.

From that point on, I had nightmares every single night, usually shortly after I'd fallen asleep. The details of the dreams themselves varied, but they all circled around themes of being hunted and killed, forgetting or losing something critically important, or being abandoned. I usually only managed between four and five hours of sleep per night. It was brutal on my mental health and Tom's too.

I imagine the lack of sleep combined with all of the other stress we were under were the main contributors to the arguments between Tom and me. We fought often throughout 2023, big fights that would build and build over days. I became extremely argumentative, stubborn, and entirely consumed by needing to control every single thing in our lives. Control was survival to me. When I wasn't in control as a little girl, I got hurt, and I refused to be hurt again. But the side effects of this strategy were incredibly destructive. I was overly emotional, mentally exhausted, and even confused at times. And I had zero self-worth. I started muttering things like, "No one needs me," "No one wants me," "My family is better off without me." I wasn't suicidal. No, this was about collapsing further and further into myself. I wanted to disappear, not off the face of the planet, but away from the pain and reality of this entire situation. The shame was just so overwhelming.

That's the mental state I was in when I went to visit Sierra in Charleston.

It was actually a family vacation. I rented this idyllic beach house for the weekend, steps from the ocean on Folly Beach. Jake, Austin,

Austin's wife, and I were planning to come down from the Charlotte area, and Sierra, who was in school at the Medical University of South Carolina in Charleston at the time, was going to stay with us out on Folly.

The past few months had been rough for my children. Austin went back to rehab in May and was not in a good place. No matter what we did, we couldn't get him to stop drinking and getting high which was causing symptoms of bipolar disorder and schizophrenia. After our vacation to Zion National Park, Sierra saw photos of Austin drinking and partying on Snapchat. When I confronted him, the conversation did not go well. My sweet son became aggressive, angry, and downright rude. I knew he was an addict, but it didn't change how hard it was to hear him speak to me that way. Sierra was appalled. She told Austin she couldn't have him in her life anymore.

By August, I was tentatively optimistic that things were actually getting better. Austin had worked hard to stay clean over the past few months, and I was hoping I could use this vacation to convince Sierra to create some space for him in her life again. Knowing she was still leery, I decided to go down earlier in the day to spend a little one-on-one time with her. We had a swanky dinner planned and then were going to hang out at the rental house waiting for the others to arrive.

We got ready like two college kids, helping each other get dressed and weighing in on hair and jewelry. We put on music and sang out loud in the mirror as we put on our makeup. I love these moments with my daughter, when I get to be more than just her mother but someone she actually sees as a friend. It was shaping up to be such a special night.

The restaurant was on the top of this high-end hotel. It was a perfect August night, the warm breeze from the ocean sweeping over the tables and kissing our skin. We chatted all the way through dinner, which was divine, and decided on dessert with espresso martinis to close out the night. Knowing Austin was headed down to join us later that night, I brought up the relationship with her brother. I told Sierra how well he had been doing and pleaded with her to just give him a chance.

Sierra was not swayed. "I've heard all of this before, Mom. We've been doing this with Austin for the past five years, and I don't believe he's miraculously changed in just a few months. I can't and won't have him in my life until he gets his shit together."

I kept pushing, asking how she could possibly abandon her brother like that. Eventually, she had had enough. "I'm not having this conversation with you anymore, Mom. I'm done." She walked away from the table to go to the bathroom, putting some physical distance between herself and the discussion to make the point.

The seconds ticked by as her heels clicked on the tile floor. Panic started to rise in my throat. I don't know what happened to me, but all I could think was, *NO! No, no, no, Sierra cannot abandon her brother!* The panic overtook my brain, and I grabbed her phone and keys out of the purse Sierra had left on the table, dumping them into my own, frantic to keep her from leaving. When she came back from the bathroom, she looked at me and said, "Where's my stuff?" confusion playing on her face. I refused to give her back her things.

I lost it, crying and pleading that she couldn't leave, couldn't turn her back on her brother. I felt like a petulant seven-year-old, except I was a grown woman vacillating between begging and being an utter bitch, the desperation and anger playing ping pong inside my head. I threw my credit card on the table, announcing, "I'm done with this shit. I'm not doing this." Sierra reached for the bill, mortified, and said, "I'll pay for it."

"No, you won't!" I snapped back. The waitress hurried over to try and help Sierra calm me down or, more likely, get me out of there. That only infuriated me more. We finally left the restaurant and retrieved my car from the valet. I drove maybe five feet and threw the car in park. I let loose on Sierra, yelling vile insults at her. She was attempting to retrieve her phone and keys from me, and I clawed back at her. At first, she was just trying to defend herself and extricate her belongings from my hiding places, but my physical attacks prompted a more vehement response from her. She screamed, "I hate you!" I hollered back, "I hate you too!" At one point, I went so far as to punch her in the head, yelling, "How could you do this to me?!?" For maybe thirty minutes, we raged, Sierra in abject disbelief as her mother turned into a violent monster before her very eyes.

I know I seemed like a monster, but I was really a seven-year-old child unleashing all of my hate and hurt and harm on a body, the only body in the vicinity. Except it was the wrong body. It was my daughter's body . . . my child, not my abuser's.

When we finally ran out of steam, I went to start the car and looked down. Sierra had scratches all over her arms. My watch was missing. I tried to drive, but I was too shaken to do so safely, so I pulled the car into a parking lot around the corner from the hotel. I wanted us to calm down and talk before we tried to drive home, but Sierra opened the car door and said she "had to get away from me."

She just started running. I scrambled out of the car after her and stood in the middle of the lot, wailing for her to come back.

It was the only time in my adult life that I actually wanted to die. If I couldn't have my daughter, I didn't want to be here. I kept pleading to the night sky, praying she could hear me, "Please, Sierra, come back. I'll be good. That wasn't the real me. I'll get help. I promise."

The thing was, I had been getting help. I was still seeing Rich, although only quarterly, and that clearly wasn't enough. What I didn't know at the time is that this was textbook post-traumatic stress disorder.[6] I was not in the driver's seat; my trauma was. But try and explain that to the adult daughter you've just physically assaulted in the parking lot of an upscale restaurant.

About twenty minutes later, Sierra came back. I hadn't moved, hoping she would see that I was not going to leave. I had called Tom to try and help me calm down, but I couldn't sit still. I got in and out of the car, pacing the lot. I was crying with my entire body, begging her not to abandon me. Sierra stood on the other side of the car from me, shaking. "I will only get back in this car if you get help, Mom." My daughter, the boundary setter. I readily agreed, so grateful she was even speaking to me that I would have promised to do anything. Sierra needed to go back to her house to grab a few things before we returned to the rental, so I drove her home. Minutes became a half hour and then an hour as I sat in the car in her driveway, staring at the light in her window, praying she would agree to come back outside and talk to me.

---

6   If you think you may be experiencing post-traumatic stress disorder, please reach out for help. You can learn more at www.ptsd.va.gov.

I know now what caused my behavior that night, but I will never forgive myself for what happened. What I did to my own daughter. As horrible as it was, it was a turning point for me. That, and the acute realization that Sierra was setting a boundary with me. I knew she was serious and that I might lose her if I couldn't get this under control. I sat in a puddle of my own tears, watch missing, arms aching, shame nearly suffocating me. I realized in that moment that I couldn't have that bitterness, that resentment, that guttural hatred in my soul anymore. I had to find a way to purge it from me or I was going to lose everyone that I loved. I really would be alone, and it would be my own fault.

Iredell County Hall of Justice. Location of the civil trial, January 29 to February 5, 2024.

12
TAKING BACK MY POWER, 2024

Three things cannot be long hidden – the sun, the moon, and the truth.
—UNKNOWN

It's funny how you can be both suffering and strengthening simultaneously. Each time I hit a new turning point along this journey, I could see how much hurt was held behind it and how much healing needed to happen. I didn't know it was possible to be overwhelmed by both at the same time.

As is typical of the court system, the trial date got bumped back twice. Don and his lawyers tried to push for another stay which meant waiting an additional six months until June 2024. After a year of trying to keep myself and my family together, I knew we wouldn't survive another six months. Jeff and I fought back hard as there was zero justification to delay it again. The trial date was finally set for January 29, 2024.

My anxiety and PTSD were so bad by the time we got to trial that I was convinced Don was going to shoot and kill me in the parking lot outside the courthouse. My nightmares were out of control and one in particular terrified me so much that I had a hard time separating the dream from reality. While asleep, I dreamed that I looked out my office window to see a white ambulance with fake American Red Cross stickers on the outside. Hooded men with machine guns were stationed all around my house. I could feel the panic rising when a car door opened, and I saw Don walking to my front door. He calmly lit my house on fire. At that point, I dropped to the floor and crawled into my kitchen knowing I was surrounded, and if I stood up, the men would shoot me. I made it to the stairs, smoke billowing in from the front of the house and raced up to my daughter's room. I could feel the heat on my skin and the bile rising in my throat as there seemed to be no way out. I ripped the sheets off of her bed and made a rope, planning to use it to get to the roof, but then what?

I woke up shaking, drenched in sweat, certain that Don had hired mercenaries to come kill me. The remnants of the dream were so real that I asked Jeff to create a plan to get me into the courthouse without having to encounter Don. I knew if I were alone in his vicinity for even a second, the panic would undo me.

Once I faced the crushing fear of just getting from the parking lot into the courtroom, I realized that the courtroom held its own injustices. No one prepared me for the humiliation of jury selection. As soon as the potential jurors entered the courtroom, my eyes started swelling. Here were fifty strangers who were about to be introduced to the secret I'd kept for fifty years. When the judge called for Don and I to stand up so he could explain the case, a fresh shame took hold, a scarlet letter put there by my brother but worn on my chest all the same. These complete strangers now knew that I had been raped. Their eyes on me made me sick to my stomach. I've never felt so small or so ashamed.

Later, I found out that the looks from some of those jurors were not pity, nor disgust, but empathy. About halfway through jury selection, one of the male jurors raised his hand. "No one's asked us if anyone close to us has been sexually assaulted. Is that important?" Up to that point, Don's attorney had only asked the jury pool if anyone had *personally* experienced a sexual assault. They clearly wanted to exclude those individuals. We couldn't believe that Don's attorneys hadn't asked the obvious next question that this gentleman alluded to, but we didn't want to tip them off to the omission either. Now that it was out in the open, Jeff went ahead and asked the question and we learned that two of the remaining three men were close to someone that had experienced sexual assault. Don's attorneys scrambled, but there was little they could do as they had accepted those jurors and passed the jury back to us. I was so appreciative of that juror for speaking up, for knowing that his experience with sexual assault was, in fact, valid, and important to this case. He wasn't the only one. Jeff and I were shocked that five of the twelve jurors and several who had been excused were the victims of sexual assault or personally knew a victim of sexual assault. I shouldn't have been surprised. A 2018 study found that 81 percent of women and 43 percent of men reported experiencing some form of sexual harassment and/or assault in their lifetime.[7] That's horrifying. I was just immensely grateful that we were going to trial with advocates in the jury box. People who understood what trauma looked like . . . and what truth looked like.

*   *   *

Coming into the trial, I knew that Wade, my ex-husband, was a witness for the other side. That's right, my ex-husband, the father of my children, testified on Don's behalf. I found out the previous spring when Don's attorneys released their witness list. The news came the same day as my son's graduation from fire school. I had to sit at lunch with Wade and his wife acting as if I wasn't about to rip his throat out. I knew he had an axe to grind with me. Our divorce had started out fairly amicable, but we inevitably fought about the kids, particularly after they turned eighteen and Wade decided that meant he had no financial responsibility for them. This was his way of getting back at me.

At the time, Wade lived in Richmond, Virginia, so he testified via video. I had reviewed the video with my attorney. There was nothing about his testimony that was particularly compelling. He even admitted I had told him that Don and David had sexually assaulted me before we got married. We expected Don's attorneys to just play the video in court as Wade was never legally subpoenaed to appear in person. I was incredulous that Wade involved himself at all, but I wasn't afraid his testimony would do much damage to our case. He was a biased witness without a lot to say.

---

7   Holly Kearl, *The Facts Behind the #metoo Movement: A National Study on Sexual Harassment and Assault* (National Sexual Violence Resource Center (NSVRC) (2018)).

At 5 p.m. the first day of the trial, I was coming out of a float spa appointment. Jury selection had been that morning, and everyone but the attorneys were released around 1 p.m. I was doing everything in my power to keep myself calm and focused. I had gotten a gift certificate for my birthday just a few weeks prior and thought a float spa might be the perfect thing to help soothe my rattled nervous system. When I pulled my phone out of my purse in the locker room, I saw that Jeff had called and texted several times. I called him back immediately. He told me that Wade was slated to testify at 9 a.m. the next morning in person on behalf of the plaintiff . . . Don. He had volunteered to drive down from Richmond to be there. That meant his video testimony remained just a deposition, and while we were prepared to address that, we had no idea what he'd say on the stand.

I started to panic. What could Wade possibly have learned in the past year that would compel him to drive down and testify against me? Wade's testimony had been recorded six months ago, in June of the previous summer. The realization hit me. "Oh my God, NO!" I screamed out loud, terror tumbling through me. Could Sierra have possibly told her father about the PTSD event in Charleston? Was Wade going to testify to that conversation as proof that I was having a nervous breakdown, that I was crazy as Don claimed? I had to know if that was the case so we could prepare. But Tom and I had decided not to tell the kids that Wade was testifying against me until after the trial. We were trying to protect them, of course, but we were also trying to protect the case, not wanting to give Wade or Don any unforeseen ammunition against me. Again, though, it seemed that our secrets were going to end up hurting them after all.

I ran to my car, hair still wet. I was crying so hard I was afraid I'd cause an accident if I tried to drive and talk. So as soon as I pulled into my neighborhood, I called Sierra. The words tumbled out of my mouth between sobs. I told her that her father was going to testify for Don and, the shame threatening to crush me, asked if she had told her father about what happened in Charleston. She assured me that she had not, but she was livid. "I can't believe this, Mom! Why did my dad do this to you? To me? To all of us? Why did he get involved in something that was absolutely NONE of his business! Mom, I don't know if I will ever be able to forgive him for this. What am I going to do?"

I urged her to do nothing for the time being. She was studying for an important final exam, and clearly, it was not her responsibility to talk sense into her father.

I will never forgive Wade for his choice to testify against me. Besides the fact that it was ineffective, it was petty, spiteful, and, I suspect, entirely motivated by his desire to get back at me. He actually said as much in an apology email he wrote to me after the trial. What I find reprehensible is his complete lack of regard for what his choice would do to his kids. Did he ever once think about how it might make them feel that their father was testifying against their mother? Particularly in a case that truly had nothing to do with him. I'll never understand it, but I have tried to lay down my anger at his choice. Not for his sake, but for mine.

*　*　*

The hits kept on coming. And not just to me, but toward my entire family. No matter what I did, I couldn't protect them from the pervasive pain this secret unlocked. On the inside, I was battered, petrified, and nearing exhaustion. But on the outside, I was determined that Don would not see me falter. If I was looking for an opponent, I'd found one, and if there was ever a time for winning, it was now.

We had some indication of the strategy Don's legal team planned to employ before the trial, but it was impossible to know exactly how they would put the pieces together until we heard them play out in court. What became clear over time is that Don's primary strategy was to try and discredit my story either by showing that I had a history of drinking and drug abuse and "untruthfulness" or to call in to question why I would have maintained a relationship with him, including letting him live in my house, if he had actually raped me. His only witnesses were himself, his wife Dee, and my ex-husband Wade, all of whom had a personal vendetta against me. It seemed like a flimsy strategy to build an entire case just on the word of these three.

Don's counsel tried to use Wade's testimony to demonstrate how untruthful I am, bringing up my so-called affair, a relationship that started *after* I told Wade I was filing for divorce, and that he found out about in marriage counseling. Wade, of course, neglected to mention his own indiscretions. I guess he thought his years of infidelity were irrelevant. Wade also admitted that he couldn't think of any other time I had been "untruthful." On cross-examination, it became particularly ironic that the witness whose role was to demonstrate my history of lying had to be repeatedly reminded of what he said during his deposition, as on the stand he stated that I had never said which brothers assaulted me. This was a direct contradiction to his earlier testimony in the video deposition and, we believe, seriously damaged his credibility with the jury.

A big part of Don's case centered around my relationship with adult Don, that is, the relationship I had with my brother after we both left our parent's house. All three of the prosecution's witnesses testified to the times we got together as a family—the Fourth of July and Memorial Day celebrations at Mom and Dad's, the Christmas and Thanksgiving get-togethers, and the invitations to participate in major life events for one of our kids. Most damning, or so they presumed, was the fact that I had let Don live with us for a period of time and that, according to them, he basically had unfettered access to my home and my kids. It was a good strategy, probably their only option, and even Jeff said that he would have pushed on the same lever if he was representing the other side.

But adult Don never raped me. When I stood up for myself at age nineteen, that part of my life ended. This Don, the one sitting up in a box with his hand on a Bible, swearing to tell the whole truth, he had become a good man. I believed that. Up until the trial, I had never feared this Don. We were never close, never friends, never siblings who enjoyed each other's company, but disowning him would have been inexcusable to my parents, particularly with no explanation. Given other circumstances, I may not have chosen to maintain a relationship with him, but in order to keep my secret, I had no choice.

What Don and his attorneys didn't do is try to prove that I was lying about the assaults. There was no witness that corroborated the claim that I was a pathological liar. No witness that said I had admitted my brothers hadn't raped me. No witness to dispute anything I had said to the witnesses to whom I had reported the same story of assault and abuse throughout my life. There was no other witness because none existed. They couldn't discredit my story because it was true.

Watching the video testimonies of the six witnesses who spoke on my behalf—girlfriends from high school and college and Rich Nisbet, my therapist—all of them recounting the times that I had painfully revealed my secret, and all of them testifying to their belief in what I told them, was overwhelmingly powerful. It buoyed me and gave me confidence that the truth rises, even fifty years later.

When I finally had my moment on the stand, it all came full circle.

As has been true my entire life, my secret weapon is preparation. I had read every word of every deposition, gone over my own testimony multiple times, practiced with Jeff in his office. I was scared shitless, but I was determined, and I knew I had the truth on my side.

When I sat down in the witness stand, I looked out and saw Don. He put his arms across his chest and started shaking his head. Before he had a chance to mouth "Liar" my way, I grabbed hold of everything inside my soul that was helping me maintain control, raised my finger to point it at him and blurted out "Don't!" with such force I surprised even myself. I hadn't said anything when he tried to intimidate me during the deposition, but I would be damned if I was going to let it go a second time around.

Startled by my outburst, Jeff quickly said "Darlene!" to get my attention. He made an "eyes on me gesture" with his fingers, a clear reminder to stay focused on him and him only. I knew I shouldn't have said anything, but the power I reclaimed in that one moment was well worth it. We began. I had to walk through every single assault one by one—the timing, the location, the details. I had already done it once during my deposition, but it was excruciating to explain everything here, in a room full of strangers, their eyes on me as I struggled to maintain composure. I held it together for the most part, but I've never once made it through the account of my assaults without crying. Knowing that, I even brought my own Kleenex up to the stand. Like I said, I was prepared.

The jury was to my left, but I was focused on Jeff, so I couldn't see their reactions. I heard a gasp when I recounted David yanking me out of the closet after I tried to hide from him. I think now about how gut-wrenching it was for me to share my trauma, but I also think about how hard it must have been for the jury to hear it. I was on the stand for almost an hour. That's a long time to sit with someone else's pain.

I was confident about my responses to Jeff's questions. As I said, we had practiced, and I knew what was coming. The cross-exam-ination was the big unknown. I knew they would try to rattle me, but I refused to give them the satisfaction of seeing me shake. When Don's attorney began, she immediately handed me a piece of paper, the volcano texts I believe. I took it with my right hand and saw the paper rattle, my hands shaking violently. To calm myself, I took a deep breath in, my mantra "I am going to win" filling my body, and let a calm breath out. I reached for the paper with my left hand and saw that my fingers and the paper were steady. I was back in control.

I know she was just doing her job, but her questions were infuri-ating. It took everything in my bones and my body not to stand up and scream, "I'm not the problem!" No, I did not bring up my childhood rapes to my ob-gyn that I started seeing when I was twenty. No, I do not recall if semen "got on me." No, I was not bleeding from my vagina prior to the age of sixteen when I first got my period. No, I did not have blood on my underwear. And no, even if I had semen or blood on my underwear, my mother would not have seen it because I did my own laundry, thank you very much. Deep breath in . . . calm breath out.

My "No's" to these questions weren't proof of anything. Don was fourteen when he raped me, barely more than a boy himself. The absence of semen or blood or permanent bodily damage belied our ages more than any absolution of guilt. This is the disgusting thing we do to victims; we make it about them. Why didn't you tell? Why wasn't there evidence?

But here's the only question that should have mattered. Why did Don rape me?

* * *

We had a hard judge for this case, but the absolute best jury.

My story is a harsh one, and Jeff had warned me from the very beginning that it was possible that the jury could find it so disturbing as to not be true. So, even though we felt like the trial had largely gone our way, when both attorneys rested their case and the judge signaled it was time for the jury to begin deliberations, I could feel the butterflies battling it out in my belly.

During the entire trial, Tom had been in the audience, watching carefully for the jury's reaction. He took notes on what they paid attention to, when they appeared bored, and what emotions played on their faces. He told us after the fact that when Don's attorney, a young female who looked barely old enough to have graduated from law school, gave her closing argument, the jury members were notably checked out. One even yawned. But when Jeff stood up, they perked up, notebooks open, pens ready. We all took that as a good sign.

The judge gave the case to the jury around 12:15. This judge was a stickler for lunch. I swear he must have had someone pass out from not eating on time because the second that clock hit noon, he would start calling for a lunch break. The jury had been deliberating for about thirty minutes when, true to form, the judge told the sheriff to go back and tell the jury we could take a break for lunch and continue deliberations this afternoon. The sheriff returned to report that the jury indicated they were almost done and just needed a few more minutes.

I turned in my seat and caught Tom's eye. He gave me a wink. Jeff had a small smile on his face too. The jury's certainty had to be because they believed me, right?

As an indication of just how strict this judge was, before he brought the jury back in the courtroom, the judge laid out a warning. "I realize this is very hotly contested. I know each side doesn't agree with the other side . . . I understand that. They [the jury] are going to come back however they come back. If it is not to your liking, I'm trusting everyone can keep their emotions in check. If you can't, I am telling you now, you can be held in contempt of court." I was already about to jump out of my skin. How could this guy expect us to have zero reaction?

Almost an hour to the minute, the jury was brought back into the courtroom. I was desperately searching their faces, looking for any sign at all of how they had decided. But to a woman, their faces were stone cold. Not a one would meet my eye. *Oh shit,* I thought to myself. *What happened? Could this really go Don's way?*

The foreman stood. The judge asked him to confirm that the jury had reached a unanimous verdict. After confirming, the foreman gave the verdict sheet to the sheriff who handed it to the judge. I watched, shaking, as the judge removed the verdict sheet. The words, "In the case of Don DeLoy against Darlene Lekowski . . ." came rolling across the courtroom like a tidal wave. I inhaled, holding my breath for what came next.

"Issue number one, did the defendant libel the plaintiff?"

"No."

"Issue two, did the defendant slander the plaintiff?"

"No."

Knowing I couldn't make a sound, I dropped my head in my hands and let the tears roll down my face. Jeff reached his arm across the seat and gently hugged my shoulders. That might have been the single best moment of my life. But it wasn't over.

"Issue seven." The second case. My countersuit. "Did the plaintiff libel the defendant?" I inhaled, holding my breath as the next word came out of the judge's mouth . . . "Yes."

My brain exploded! I looked up, tears pouring down my face, and mouthed "Thank you" to the jurors who could see me. It was such an insufficient gesture, but it was all I could offer at the moment, and I sent my entire heart with it. Some of them nodded their acknowledgement, still stone faced as they were instructed to remain. But I needed them to know what they had just done for me. What they had just done for little Darlene.

Redemption. All of that pain, all of that suffering, all of the nightmares, the therapy, the preparation. They all paid off. Because the truth was on my side. Over and over again, all I could think was, *Oh my God! We did it! We won!*

I was later told that the jury made a unanimous decision on both cases within minutes of being handed the case. The remainder of the hour was for them to decide how much money to award me. While Don had asked for a half million dollars in damages in his suit against me, in my counter suit, I specified that it should be up to the jury to award what they felt was appropriate for what I'd been through.

Between actual and punitive damages—$210,000. That's what they felt I was owed. That's how much damage they could see Don's inability to own the truth and his assertion that I was the one who was lying had done to me.

The judge released the jury shortly thereafter which I was heartbroken about as I had wanted an opportunity to thank them in person. The judge let the rest of us go, but he called the attorneys into chambers. When Jeff rejoined us, he told us that the judge wanted us to come back after lunch and attempt to finalize the award. He wanted both sides to consider what they would settle for so this did not have to go on and on in the courts.

At lunch, my little rag-tag crew was ecstatic! We were high fiving, hugging, and crying happy tears for once. This had never been about the money for me, and while I felt like Don owed me something for the hell he'd put me through, Tom and I were willing to settle for $100,000. The important thing is that we had won, that a jury of my peers believed me, and that justice was finally, finally being done.

We returned to the courtroom ready to discuss settling, but the judge never said anything about it. Apparently, Don's attorney had told him during the break that Don was unwilling to negotiate and would file an appeal instead. Not surprising, but frustrating all the same.

When the supplemental judgment was finally settled three months later, our judge held firm on what the jury had awarded me. Don officially owed me the $210,000 plus interest. I had also requested consideration for my legal fees, seeing as how I had not been the one to bring this suit to the court in the first place. In a civil case in North Carolina, the judge determines if there is a statutory basis for attorney's fees to be awarded and, if so, to whom. I wonder if our judge might have been a little frustrated with Don himself, because in his supplemental judgment, he ruled that almost $40,000 in costs and attorney's fees were also Don's responsibility.

I couldn't help but smirk. Checkmate.

2025. My family today, *clockwise from top left:*
Tom, Austin, Jake, Sierra, Karlita, Me

Epilogue

I won.

It's what I thought I wanted. A happy ending. Justice finally served. Turns out, winning the lawsuit against me and my countersuit against Don was just the beginning. The trial broke open something in me. I thought that if I won, I could finally be free. That if the jury agreed with me, it would be the validation I needed. That if Don was finally held accountable for what he did to me, the world would right itself and my healing would be complete. It turns out that healing isn't that linear or righteous.

One of the things that has brought me the most shame in my life is that the night Don assaulted me in my bed, I froze. My parents were right downstairs. Why didn't I scream? Why didn't I fight? The hot heat of shame I experienced on the stand trying to defend my actions that night was nothing compared to the hell I've put myself through trying to figure out why I did nothing. But, as I've begun to lean in to being a survivor of sexual trauma and abuse, I've been exposed to a wealth of research I had no idea existed. Turns out, current literature suggests that fight and flight are not the only *f's* that describe how humans respond in the midst of trauma. There are actually multiple *f's*, with, you guessed it, freeze, being well-recognized amongst them.[8,9] Understanding that my reaction was a trauma response and that freezing is, in fact, a *normal* reaction to trauma helped me accept that no matter what my head said, my body was innately doing what it felt like it needed to protect itself from danger.

There's nothing shameful about that. That's called survival.

Throughout the trial, I was plagued by negative thoughts. How much money I was spending on legal fees, what this would do to my family, whether or not I'd be better off just disappearing. The negativity was pervasive and an incredible strain on the limited energy I had. At the time, I was undergoing a therapy called EFT (emotional freedom technique) tapping. Recognizing that the negativity was overwhelming my system, my life coach, Molly Purvines, suggested that we reframe my thinking. We started with the way I was approaching the legal fees. Instead of seeing it as a tremendous strain on me and my family, we worked together to reframe that way of thinking to: This

---

8   H. Stefan Bracha, "Freeze, Flight, Fight, Fright, Faint: Adaptationist Perspectives on the Acute Stress Response Spectrum," *CNS Spectrums* 9, no. 9 (2004): 679-85, doi:10.1017/s1092852900001954.

9   Carmit Katz et al., "Beyond Fight, Flight, and Freeze: Towards a New Conceptualization of Peritraumatic Responses to Child Sexual Abuse Based on Retrospective Accounts of Adult Survivors," *Child Abuse & Neglect* 112, 104905 (2021), doi:10.1016/j.chiabu.2020.104905.

is the cost of the truth. I could be okay with that, and the subtle shift totally changed my energy around it. Taking it one step further, I added a reminder on my calendar. It pops up every Friday morning to this day. It reads: "I am open to the legal fees being paid in miraculous and unexpected ways." That message took so much stress off of me. And it changed the way I approached everything, freeing me up to be open to what could be possible instead of what felt impossible.

Ultimately, the entirety of my healing journey became about letting go. First and foremost, I had to let go of the fact that Don is never going to take responsibility for what he did to me. Not for raping me, not for dividing our family, not for putting me on trial, and not for paying me the damages awarded by the jury. I am never going to get an apology from him, the only thing I actually wanted and felt I deserved. And I have had to let that go so that I can continue to heal.

Throughout my life, I thought I needed to win in order to be loved and believed. I held on to the fact that I won the lawsuit and my countersuit as proof of my worthiness, but ultimately, I had to let that go too. Winning is not the pathway to worth, and while validating, it has changed nothing about what happened to me or what will happen for me moving forward.

I had to let go of other beliefs too, postulates that had been the guiding forces in my life but no longer served me: I have to be in control. I did it alone then, I can do it alone now. Silence means safety. I must survive.

I want my life to be about more than just survival. I've spent so many years with a death grip on the reins of my existence, certain that letting loose just a bit would result in more trauma, more pain, more hurt. But, to truly honor the relationships I treasure most, with

Tom and my children, I had to learn to open my hands and my heart and trust that they've got me. Don't get me wrong, my fingers are always poised to snap shut at any given moment, and stress will bring me back to that place quickly, but at least now I can recognize it as a coping mechanism, not a life strategy.

My life now is so much richer. For most of my years, I felt like I've lived parallel existences, the Darlene who carries this enormous secret, and the Darlene who pretends like nothing bad ever happened. Finally, I am a whole person, living one life. A life I am deeply grateful for.

My parents are both deceased now. They died without ever knowing what happened to me. I succeeded in keeping the secret from them, from sparing them that pain, and myself the pain of their inadequate response. My mother's death still haunts me, but the more I relinquish the guilt over her dying alone, the more I'm able to be at peace with her passing. Letting my dad go was extremely hard, but I was not at war with myself. I know I did all that I could for him. I was at his side, holding his hand as he took his last breath. My brothers always threatened that if I told, I would be an orphan. Oddly enough, now I am. As a child, that prospect was terrifying; as an adult, it's an unfortunate phase of life. But the finality of it never leaves me. My opportunity, if I had ever wanted one, to tell them what happened to me is gone. It is done. And I have to be okay with the way I played it.

I no longer have a relationship with either David or Don. Our family has gone from a set of seven to just two, Dale and I. I'm still grappling with that as my whole motivation for keeping the secret all these years was to keep the family I had together. I guess the truth has a way of exposing relationships that need to end.

While I've lost much of my family of origin, the family I created for myself is thriving. My children continue to amaze me with their strength and resiliency, and with the kind of people they are becoming in this world. All of these years, I thought I was protecting them by keeping my secret, but the price I paid for that silence showed up in every one of my interactions with my children. Opening up about what happened to me was like turning on a light in a dim room.

After learning about my abuse, Jake, my son, said, "Mom, I never understood why you were always in my business. Now, I get it. I get you." Survival is something Jake can understand. As a child, he was always smaller and quieter than Austin, and he was bullied for it as a result. It has affected who he is and what he's chosen to do as a result, so knowing *why* I was the way I was as his mother mattered to him.

Austin still has a hard time talking about or reading about my abuse. It's triggering for him. Having dealt with his own mental demons, he knows that kind of pain, and it's difficult for him to recognize the anguish I was dealing with even while he was in the midst of his own suffering. In the three years since our family staged an intervention with Austin, he has turned his life around. No more marijuana, no more alcohol. As a result, the voices in his head have quieted, and my tender-hearted son has returned.

Sierra, the best of any of us with boundaries, bluntly told me that if I didn't get help, I wouldn't have a relationship with her. I'm so proud of that kid. Who says that to their own mother? But, she had every right to. After that horrible night in Charleston, I connected with a therapist, a psychiatrist, and started seeing Molly for EFT tapping. I also increased the frequency of my therapy sessions with Rich, even going so far as to fly to Tennessee for treatment, which is where he now practices. Investing in my own healing with the right kind of help has made a world of difference. As a result, I haven't had a PTSD episode since that night. Sierra has extended grace I'm not sure I would have been able to give. She is slowly beginning to trust me again, and I will be forever grateful for that second chance.

And Tom? Well, Tom is still my Viking, always trying to protect me. He's not the letting-go type, but he sees that my ability to let go is directly related to my capacity to lean in. And he likes that part very much.

I still have nightmares several times a week, but they are different. Weaker. They are no longer full of fear and terror around being raped or murdered. No longer do I see red flames or rats or spiders on my curtains. The one dream I can't shake is that I've forgotten to do something important and as a result I've lost everything. I sit up in bed in a panic, yell, and shed a couple of tears, but Tom helps calm me down, and I go back to sleep with no memory of the episode the next morning. I'm much more likely now to curl toward Tom and hold his hand while I sleep, occasionally patting his body for reassurance. On a recent overnight trip with my daughter, I did the same thing. Grasping her hands while I slept, taking comfort in the touch of my first born.

Of all the things I have done to help myself heal, the process of putting down my story in this memoir may have been the most transformational. Yes, I had to relive the darkest moments of my trauma, but this time for a purpose. The more I shared what happened to me, the less I cried, not because it was any less painful but because I could finally integrate what happened *to me* with what became *of me*. Writing this book allowed me to reach back and take the hand of my younger self, the little Darlene who was assaulted, afraid, and alone. I am pulling her forward, using her story to reach out to others who have experienced the same trauma to give them a voice as well.

I never thought I would become an advocate. It's hard to believe you'll advocate for something you never own for yourself. But, once my secret became public, I knew I couldn't let this end with me. While underreported, it is believed that sibling sexual abuse is the most common form of intrafamilial child sexual abuse.[10] There are thousands of little Darlenes out there. I can't leave them assaulted, afraid, and alone. It is time to speak up, speak out, and create environments within families and within our communities where sibling sexual trauma and abuse do not carry the shame and stigma it did for me. In doing so, we can honor and protect the voices of children brave enough to tell and encourage others to do the same, knowing that they will never be alone.

It's also time for resilience to be seen as the superpower it truly is. Resilience is more than just survival. Resilience is the grit that keeps empowering us to stand back up even when it would be far easier to lay on the ground. I am a survivor, yes, but I am also one resilient son of a bitch who fought with everything I had to become a healthy, whole person. I want to celebrate that. I *deserve* to celebrate that. And I want to inspire others to celebrate their own resiliency, to know that healing from trauma is nothing short of heroic.

I didn't ask for this. The second half of my life was not slated for public speaking and advocacy work. But, when Don sued me, he unknowingly gave me a gift. His actions forced me to finally let it all

---

10   Yates and Allardyce, *Sibling Sexual Abuse* (2021).

go. I'll never understand his motivation. For assaulting me in the first place, for suing me, for not settling. I never wanted to destroy Don's life; all I ever wanted was an apology. But once it was clear that he was not going to back down, I did want to win. I *had* to win, and I thought that would bring me justice. But justice looks different to me now.

What I won was the validation from a jury of my peers. What I won was the ability to freely tell my story. What I won was the ability to let it go.

Justice is not winning. It never was. Justice is being freed from the burden of my secret.

*   *   *

When I first started writing this book, I came across the origin story of Pandora's box. I had a vague understanding of what the metaphor meant in common vernacular, but had never heard the back story of the popular phrase.

In the legend of Pandora's box, the god Zeus confined all of the suffering that could befall mankind—sickness, pain, deceit, desertion, isolation, war—into a single vessel and sent it to Pandora as a gift, knowing that her curiosity about the contents would lead her to unleash the horrors held within on humanity. One day, unwise to the contents of the vessel, Pandora did just as Zeus expected: She opened the box, letting loose the evils contained within to attack the unsuspecting human world. Desperate to stop the flood, she slammed the box closed.

Except Zeus had hidden another gift inside. Concealed on the lid of the box, accessible only if the box was open, was the final gift.

Hope.

I had my own box of evils. And like Pandora, I kept it closed for fear of what it would do to those I loved the most. But little did I know that the one thing I needed was also trapped inside the box, and it was only when it was opened by force that the gift, the final gift, could be released.

Open the box. Let it all go. You can't control the evil. But you can give hope a chance.

Acknowledgments

To my Viking, my husband Tom: You held my hand through the darkest nights with unwavering strength and fierce devotion. Your love, courage, and steady presence carried me when I could not walk alone. You are my rock, my refuge, and the proof that healing through love is possible.

To my children Sierra, Jake, and Austin, and daughter-in-law Karlita: Thank you for living through the weight of a mother with trauma and for supporting me in ways only you could. Each of you, in your own beautiful way, helped me find the light again. Your love, loyalty, and presence gave me the strength to move forward, to heal, and to begin again.

To my brother Dale: Like me, you never asked for any of this. You were the innocent brother who never once hurt or betrayed me. Growing up you were my hero in so many ways. I devote this story to us and the family struggles we endured. Thank you for loving me and believing in me, always.

To Jessica Buchanan & Soul Speak Press: From the beginning, you heard my truth and believed in the power of telling it. As a trauma survivor yourself, you understand the necessity of giving a voice to women whose stories have been buried too long. You gave voice to the girl who was silenced, and you helped me step fully into the woman who now speaks. I cannot describe how much I appreciate you and your company.

To my co-author Jess Greenwood: Words will never be enough to express how endlessly grateful I am that Soul Speak Press brought us together. You became my witness, my translator, and my steady companion on the most vulnerable journey of my life. You didn't just listen—you truly heard me. You held space for the raw, the broken, and the tangled truths I carried. In my panic and tears, your objectivity was a gift, challenging me to see my story with clarity when fear threatened to blur it. You never flinched, never rushed, never imposed. Instead, you met me exactly where I was, and step by step, we shaped this story together. Jess, because of you, this book is told with such clarity and strength. Because of you, my truth and purpose to help others will now forever be told. For that, and you, I am forever grateful.

To Jeff Kuykendal: Thank you for standing beside me with unwavering dedication through the trial and beyond. You have no idea how much I appreciated how you treated me as an equal, a partner and not just a client. You gave me respect, strength, and the confidence to face my attacker and enable the jury to hear the truth. Because of your steadfast legal guidance and expertise, justice prevailed. The impact you've had on my life goes far beyond winning the case. You helped me reclaim my voice and move forward with strength. I simply cannot thank you enough.

To Mark Weaver: Thank you for seeing my random post on our neighborhood Facebook page and recognizing a friend in need.

Without hesitation, you connected me to Jeff Kuykendal, a referral that changed everything. Your kindness and quick action led me to the support I needed to face one of the most difficult trials of my life—and succeed.

To my girlfriends: You have been my lifeline through so many phases of my life. To all who have stood by me—and especially to Susan, Peggy, Tina, Brenda, and Dianna, who bravely testified for me—I will never have enough words to thank you. You never gave up on me when life felt too heavy for me to hold on. You saw my pain, believed me, and never let me forget that I wasn't walking this road alone. Your courage to stand beside me was the show of strength I needed to ensure justice was realized. I will never forget what you did and I am forever bound to you in gratitude and sisterhood.

To Rich Nisbet, Owner, Above It All 360: For over twenty years, you've been my steady place to land—guiding me through the traumatic memories I thought would break me and fears I believed I'd never escape. Before you, I was ready to give up, but your processes helped me learn how to manage them when no one else could. When the trial brought everything crashing back, you stood by me still— offering courage and truth in your testimony. Because of your insight, patience, and care, I was able to find myself again. I will always be forever grateful I found you. You are not only my counselor but also a dear friend.

To Molly Purvines, Owner, The AHA! Coach: From the moment we met, I felt seen and safe with you. When I was newly diagnosed with PTSD in 2023, you gently showed me a way forward through EFT tapping. You helped me understand that nightmares and PTSD reactions didn't mean I was broken. That fear could loosen its grip, and that peace was still possible for me. Session by session, you gave me the tools to breathe again, to steady myself, and to believe I could heal. Because of you, I carry a resilience I never thought I'd find. I am forever grateful our paths crossed.

To the jury: How I wish I could have thanked each of you in person for what you gave me that day—something beyond measure. You listened to the facts, you heard my truth, and with your unanimous verdict, you gave me back my voice. Thank you for truly seeing me, for believing me, and for giving me justice when it mattered most. I will carry the deepest gratitude for each of you in my heart, always.

To Judge Albright: Thank you for presiding over my trial with both toughness and fairness. You upheld the law with integrity. Your steady commitment to justice gave me the chance to be heard and vindicated. I am deeply grateful for your professionalism, discernment, and the dignity you brought to the process.

To Graham Morgan: Thank you for walking with me through every page of this memoir, offering not just your legal expertise but also your patience and care. Knowing you were making sure my truth could be told safely lifted a heavy weight from me. Your thoughtful guidance, availability, and protection gave me the confidence to share what needed to be said. I am profoundly grateful for the way you safeguarded both my story and my voice.

To the millions who were sexually abused and silenced: I hear you. I believe you. I see you. Together, we will shatter the silence and reclaim our voices. Though these pages are written from my life, this story belongs to us all.

RESOURCES

If you or someone you love has experienced sexual abuse or trauma, please know—you are not alone. Healing is possible, and support is out there. The following resources offer insight, guidance, and a community for survivors, their families, and allies.

These are just a starting point. I continue to add more resources on my website, www.darlene-lekowski.com, as I discover organizations, practices, and communities that are making a difference for me and for others. Wherever you are in your journey, may you find comfort, courage, and connection in knowing others walk beside you.

Sibling Sexual Trauma & Abuse (SSTA) Resources:
The following organizations and communities focus on sibling sexual trauma and abuse (SSTA). They provide education, advocacy, and support for survivors, families, professionals, and advocates. It is my hope this list will continue to grow as more voices come forward about this hidden form of sexual abuse—one that is far too common, yet too often overlooked.

- **5WAVES (US)** – 5WAVES.org. A survivor-led nonprofit raising awareness and offering resources for those impacted by sibling sexual trauma worldwide.
  - » **Sibling Sexual Trauma** – www.siblingsexualtrauma.com. Provides education, tools, and advocacy for survivors and families affected by sibling abuse.
- **SSTA Aware (US)** – www.sstaaware.org. Raising awareness and supporting healing for survivors of sibling sexual trauma.
- **Incest AWARE (International)** – www.incestaware.org. International advocacy dedicated to ending incest and intrafamilial sexual violence.
- **#SiblingsToo (Canada)** – www.siblingstoo.com. Conversations and survivor stories that break the silence on sibling sexual trauma.
- **SAARA** – www.unh.edu/saara. The Sibling Aggression and Abuse Research and Advocacy Initiative at the University of New Hampshire is dedicated to raising awareness about all forms of sibling abuse and providing resources and training to professionals, parents, and survivors.
- **SSTA Online Peer Support Groups:**
  - » 5WAVES Discord Survivor Community – Online peer support group with separate spaces for survivors, parents, and friends. Email info@5WAVES.org for information on how to join.
  - » Empower Survivors Facebook Peer Support Group for Survivors of Sibling Childhood Sexual Abuse – www.facebook.com/groups/646423866554980.

A private online space for survivors of sibling childhood sexual abuse to connect and share experiences.

Additional Sexual Abuse Resources:

- **Brave Step** – www.bravestep.org. A nonprofit dedicated to strengthening the well-being of adults and communities impacted by sexual violence through therapy, education, and empowerment programs for survivors, loved ones, and allies.
- **Saprea** – www.saprea.org. Saprea exists to liberate individuals and society from child sexual abuse and its lasting impacts. While headquartered in Utah, they serve survivors throughout the US.
- **Thriving Survivors (UK)** – www.thrivingsurvivors.co.uk. Offers therapy, peer support, and training for survivors of sexual trauma and their loved ones.

Healing Methods that Worked for Me

- **Grounding & Breathing Techniques**
  Simple somatic practices like mindful breathing, looking around me, and staying present helped me stay stable during my trial and whenever I feel triggered.
- **Above It All 360 – Rich Nisbet, Owner and Counselor –** www.aboveitall360.com
  After trying many traditional approaches, working with Rich Nisbet finally allowed me to release the hidden weight of past trauma by uncovering long-buried conclusions from childhood that were still shaping my life. His unique process blends guided self-discovery, precise questioning,

and practical direction that quickly bypass surface-level discussions and get to the actual source of emotional pain. Rather than circling around old wounds, Rich helps people confront what is real, dissolve what no longer serves them, and regain clarity, strength, and control over their own lives. The result is fast, lasting relief and a renewed sense of freedom and determination.

- **The AHA! Coach – Molly Purvines, Owner and Life Coach** – www.theahacoach.net
  When I was diagnosed with PTSD in 2023, EFT (emotional freedom technique) became a lifeline. Through tapping, I was able to release emotions trapped in my body and begin restoring balance and freedom from my trauma.